IN BOLIVIA

JEFFREY S. JENKINS

IN BOLIVIA

Copyright © Jeffrey S. Jenkins, 2009.

All rights reserved. No part of this book may be used or reproduced in any manner whatsoever without written permission except in the case of brief quotations embodied in critical articles or reviews.

ISBN: 978-0-578-03319-8

"Bolivia. Unida, Grande, y para Todos."

-Evo Morales Campaign Banner

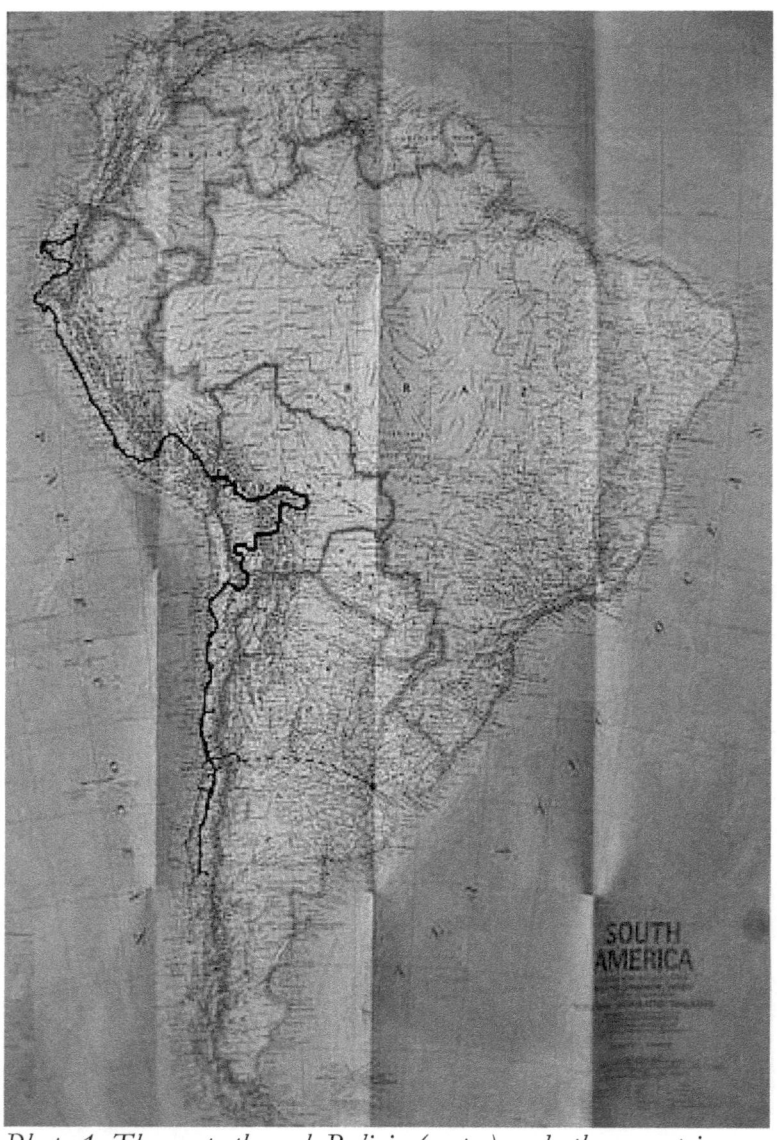

Photo 1: The route through Bolivia (center) and other countries.

Table of Contents

1. Leaving Chile..7
2. Enter the Altiplano..14
3. The Mountain that Eats Men.......................................32
4. Ginger's Paradise..44
5. Spider Monkeys and Pejerreyes..................................57
6. Cochabamba..76
7. The Peace...92
8. Inca Origin...110
9. Epilogue: Back in the States......................................128

1. Leaving Chile

My time was done in Santiago. I would soon be heading to the Great North, or Norte Grande as the Chileans called their northern frontier, and up into Bolivia where I would begin a solo backpacking journey through South America for the next couple months. I'd been up all night packing and spending time with Chilean friends who I vowed to come back and visit. But I knew it would be hard to get back to Chile, given my wanderlust for places new and different.

It started when I left my first post-college job and came to Chile to teach K-12 English. I taught a class for every grade level each week and kept busy with song and dance lesson plans for the younger students, or political discussions, in the absence of a structured classroom, for the adolescents. It was challenging work but usually less rigorous than the sardine-can-like conditions I faced on the Metro de Santiago transit system in order to get to the school.

Now, I enjoyed the view from my apartment one last time. It was night and I stood on the newly completed sunroof feeling the looming presence of the giant white Virgin Mary statue that topped the nearby Cerro San Cristobal hill. She was lit up at night over the dark cerro, which made it seem as if she floated in the sky, watching over the city. In front of me was a skyscraper shaped like a giant cell phone standing alone in this barrio of Santiago. The country's tallest skyscraper housed Telefonica; the country's largest telecommunications company.

My roommate Chris and I had petitioned for the last four months we lived in that apartment to have a banister or railing built to guard against any accidental falls from the sunroof, which was five stories above the ground. Only on our last day of living there was it finally constructed. Luckily, in the course of all the parties we'd hosted, no one managed to be dumb enough to peer over the edge, lose their footing or trip over their untied shoelaces, and fall off. Though, it was probably because of the excessive pigeon guano that made for a nice layer of paste over the deck. If anyone ever falls off that deck I'm sure they'll be doing so without the unbreakable bond of shoe sole to pigeon guano to lumber, which would otherwise save them. Surely everyone we had over at that place tied their shoes in double knots. This was a method I had naively thought to be uniquely American, taught in early schooling to avoid tripping over one's laces. I soon saw the double knot-tying present on the shoes of the kindergarten students I was instructing in Chile. I was now sure, anthropologically speaking, that the ontological reasons behind double knot-tying arose from disparate origins in the evolution of human social survival mechanisms. That is, unbeknown to Americans, Chileans were teaching their kids a method to double up their laces so as to avoid falling off buildings like this one, which was covered in a blanket of pigeon crud. Even more, this unique form of social Darwinism seemed to evolve symbiotically with that of pigeons that decided to lay their guano droppings on habitable human spaces. I confirmed this fact whenever I saw a pigeon arrive on the roof expressly to defecate when it had anywhere else in the city to do so! There was much to miss.

◎ ◎ ◎

The next day I was on a bus that carried me to San Pedro de Atacama, where I would spend one final day in Chile. The town was dry and dead, and from what I heard, culturally more Bolivian than Chilean. I set out to secure a place for later that night and found a small hostel room with an Irish guy I'd met from the bus. It was still the morning and we went to find a tour guide to show us around the area.

Coarse sand passed through my toes as the mass of tourists, including myself, ascended the massive sand dune. The sun was setting when we reached the top of the dune. I looked back and saw a moonscape of wind-whipped rock formations. Here, in the Valley of the Moon and the nearby Valley of the Dead, Salvador Dali's painted surrealist landscapes seemed more like a poor impressionist depiction of what was actually lying before my eyes. The Atacama Desert in Chile receives the lowest amount of rainfall anywhere in the world. My tour guide was in his late twenties, and I was sure he'd probably only dreamed about water falling from the sky.

We retired to the tourist-soaked village of San Pedro de Atacama and spent our evening with other parched travelers. The local government rationed water use. But if you ever decide to visit and miss your shower, don't worry, because geyser tours leave a couple hours before sunrise. There's no better way to watch the sun come up.

On the next day I was up at the crack of dawn with my travel friends to start what would be a three-day trek by SUV across Bolivia's high-altitude desert. It would be three days until we'd reach the first town in Bolivia but only hours until we would cross the border from Chile.

I had my first llama sighting only a few kilometers past the Chilean border or what my lack of knowledge conceded to be the general border region. We were climbing 2,000 meters higher than the 2,500 we were at: a 2,000-meter ascent over 60 kilometers. It was an arid expanse of plains – the great Bolivian Altiplano. The landscape was dotted with bushy but flat scrub grass. I looked into the distance and squinted to see over the hills, they seemed to reach for the sky with limitless peaks. My field of vision became distorted with the blue sky above as my only limit to dwarf the mundane grandeur. I think it was perhaps the bluest sky I'd seen to date. I was no longer capable of discerning a five-foot tall llama from a three-foot tall scrub bush. They seemed to be made out of the same fibrous material built to withstand such unrelenting frigidity that was pervasive throughout this environ. The scrub bush was getting thicker; it was like a green quilt lying over the mountain, ripped haphazardly in some places to expose pockets of rock, while a more purposeful tear in the blanket revealed the gravel road ahead. These scrub bushes no longer looked like the brown llamas but rather like the pointed green tops of a thousand troll heads waiting to emerge from their nascent sleep underground. You know...those trolls that were popular in the late 80's, with their wavy neon hair? I was sure that at night they were intent on teasing the slumbering cameloids, lifting up their floppy ears and whispering ideas of rebellion against the tourists. When day came again, the trolls would revert back to their vegetative state and the llamas would be left in silent puzzlement. You and I can clearly see this confusion on their lopsided faces. They apparently just chew grass, but little do we know of their cover, due to a llama-to-human linguistic barrier. The trolls work tirelessly in order to condition the llamas to withstand human tourist invasion of their land. If you looked as ugly as a llama wouldn't you want to stop all the pictures and fanfare? At least the llamas were used to this altitude and could handle it better than I could. I hadn't become delusional yet, only borderline fantastical.

    We passed the Bolivian checkpoint and were given immigration cards to fill out for our three-day SUV trek. An abandoned bus sat across from the small outpost that flew a Bolivian flag. The banner flapped with each wind gust. Evidently the border was unmarked and I'd been in Bolivia for what seemed to be the last hour of transport. I walked over to the bus and saw a small zorro pup (much like a fox but funnier looking with its bush tail and big ears) chase its sibling around in circles. Sensing an *Into the Wild* moment I used all the abdominal strength I could muster at the altitude and pulled myself on top of the rusted bus then slowly spun round, trying to take in the whole panorama. I had no idea where my next destination would be; I only knew it would be unknown and that was the most reassuring thought. Now, I was going into the wild...I was going into Bolivia!

Photo 2: Scrub bush near the Chilean-Bolivian border.

2. Enter the Altiplano

Bitter; the coca tea we were drinking. The coarse highland, inland, no man should be in this land-kinda-air. Seven of us piled under seven llama wool blankets each. Forty nine blankets in total. Someone heard reports of -15 degrees Celsius at night. By day I saw what was one of the most vivid and stark landscapes I'd ever experienced. Crayola must make their red crayons here. Every hue of red in the color spectrum emerged from Laguna Colorada. By night, the concrete walls of what the tour company dubbed a 'hostel' exuded the foul stench of sulfur. The only other option for lodging within a 400-kilometer radius was the adjoining sheep shed, but for sleeping I decided on the native, dead wool over that of the more lively denizens outback.

The day was a journey through several environments which were all high and cold. Now I was sitting in a 'hostel' which some might call an 'emergency survival structure', anticipating the night of frozen hell that so many travelers had forewarned me about. "Ya the Salar de Uyuni was great – the whole trip, from the Dali-esque rock structures to the thousands of flamingos lining the multi-chromatic lagoons. Except for the night we had to survive negative temperatures with nothing but a few blankets." This was a common description I'd heard of the three-day crossing. In a room with seven beds, I foolishly chose the one that was by the window. We froze our asses off in confirmed -15 degrees Celsius temperatures at four and a half kilometers above sea level (ASL), or roughly three miles ASL, on the frigid altiplano. I can honestly say that it was the coldest night I'd ever endured, though I remember that one night that did come close.

When I was in Boy Scouts at the age of 13, I went up to Mount Rainier with my troop and built an igloo to sleep in. Keep in mind that Mount Rainier is where climbers in the contiguous United States go to train for Everest. Now, see, my particular igloo-building group didn't completely finish our shelter. We were the least experienced and had built a structure that exceeded the maximum 6-foot diameter that was needed for structural integrity of the dome shape. This, of course, was the most highly-stressed detail of the many training sessions the Scout Masters gave.

We didn't finish the igloo and were forced to split up and sleep in another group's snow dome rather than freeze outside. Half of us split for one of the leaders' cars. But I refused to do this; I wanted a legitimate igloo experience. So I was relegated to another, smaller igloo with more people. I anticipated a rather uncomfortable night, as I'd be sleeping on ice, crammed between several other sweaty boys in sub-freezing conditions. Though I must concede that it was one of the warmer nights I've had outdoors. Forget what you've seen in *Nanook of the North* – a true igloo is built with a recessed entrance that comes up into the dome in order to trap body heat. This made for an incredibly cozy night, except that I was awaken by a full bladder only to realize that my boots were frozen rock solid. I had neglected to sleep with my boots within my sleeping bag as my mother had suggested. Alternatively, as I think back on it, I'm really not sure if the collection of boots in the entrance kept in the heat, but to this day I concede to my Mom's advice solely because of this experience. Either way, I was so warm that I woke up sweating.

Now, I was in a permanent structure, and though it wasn't made of ice it was less reliable in sheltering me from the adverse conditions of temperature, altitude, remoteness, and being a foreigner. The night of the igloo had been around 11 degrees Fahrenheit or about -11 in Celsius — still warmer than -15 degrees Celsius. I was about a mile and a half higher in Bolivia. On Mount Rainier we could easily find a ranger via the park service in 15 minutes, whereas in this remote corner of South America it was about a day's journey by SUV to the closest post. Most importantly, the igloo was built on U.S. soil (or snow) and there in that shelter I was still unregistered with the Bolivian Naturalization Service. Lacking any climatically reasonable location to station a border crossing, the government was fine with letting us wait a few days to legally enter.

Did I mention that I was sleeping next to the only window? I quickly recruited everyone's extra towels to place in front of the paper-thin glass. I used the ruse that it would be the best way to trap in heat for the betterment of the group.

Further debates throughout the night included the following: to drink wine or not; whether our fellow teacher, Carrie, had projectile vomited due to the altitude or from potential yellow fever; if we should subsequently get help for Carrie; if the alcohol was helping us or hindering acclimatization efforts; and who really had the most layers on? You could only fold a piece of paper eight times, but was there a limit to how many layers of clothing one could physically wear? Stephanie won easily with 11 layers. Eventually a Quechua mountain man came in with a small cup of coca leaves soaked in hot water with copious amounts of sugar. Result: ya, this stuff really did help Carrie, but we remained unsure if the wine, ibuprofen, and various incantations had an equal effect.

Everyone went to sleep and the story would usually end here, but this wasn't the case because there was too little oxygen or heat to sleep comfortably. I thought that sleeping would only lead me to dream about a cozy warm bed where I could breathe fully by a cobblestone fire place. Perhaps this was the only sensible thing that my body could do to cope with the severe conditions. But this, in fact, sent me in to complete panic. If dreaming could be that nice then would I somehow forget about the world around me and slip into a permanent slumber? As I lay on the slab flat bed munching my coca leaves, my face sticking out from underneath the blanket and consuming water every ten minutes, I could hear Stephanie humming *Cocaine* by Clapton.

Thinking in an asynchronous state due to my heightened awareness from the coca and lowered stamina from the altitude, I realized that I should head to the bathroom to rid myself of any excess liquids lest I need to wake up at five in the morning to relieve myself under even colder conditions. When I arrived in the room I settled back into my bed and lay supine. I heard faint murmurs and then laughs from the native family in the room next-door, trading stories of the tourists' naiveté over lantern light. As I tried to shift my focus away from an ever-growing headache, my ears became more attuned to the faint coughs, gasps, and jerky bodily movements of my travel mates. I took solace in the fact that all seven of us were enduring the same frozen hell. My fears of air exhaustion and bitter coldness were eventually abated as I became more cognizant of the fact that everyone else was in the same situation. I fell asleep to the whispers from next door and my fellow strugglers' grunts, only to awaken into a dream scape where thousands of turf-haired trolls cautiously extolled plots of Andean upheaval into the ears of snoring llamas whose only sign of recognition were muffled grunts.

I woke up groggy and approached our guide who was fixing the SUV. The guide, Edgar, asked how I felt. I answered with a more or less tired – "Cansado, mas o menos." I'd been riding with him in the front seat for most of the trip. I liked being up there with the guide and experiencing things through his vantage point, seeing him shift gears, put on his sunglasses and readjust his seat as we head over a bumpy segment. I stared out at the vast blood-red Laguna Colorada to watch seagulls cry above their long-lost ocean. All that remained were large piles of salt and borax. I looked around and saw local girls pass, and I exchanged smiles with them as they strolled by in their traditional garb. These teenage mountain princesses let the sheep out to be fed while their mom calmed the squawks of the seagulls with her leftover bread. As I watched the remains of our breakfast go to the seagulls and heard the tiny, almost doll-like baby lambs *bah* to their mothers for food, I realized that it was all a cycle. See, we ate cheese last night on our pasta. What I thought was llama cheese must have been from some other animals these people were housing at their remote compound. The sheep meandered across a dusty road with the gulls pecking in between them. Every day a new set of SUVs will arrive and will leave fresh tracks in the otherwise pristine, arid landscape. Another set of eyes will discover the beauty in this remote, harsh landscape. I had awoken to a beautiful day and after Edgar was done trying to fix our radiator I corrected myself by telling Edgar, "Me desperté," or, "I'm awake".

◎ ◎ ◎

Photo 3: The water tower in the unnamed/unmapped ghost town.

I sat on a woven wicker chair, watching the sunset over the Salar de Uyuni. Dogs were playing together, our Land Rovers were parked, and more were pulling up over dis-contiguous and ever shifting piles of dust. Upon arriving at the hostel we had to wait for the first rooms to reach full occupancy before the staff would turn on the heater for the hot water. Everyone was in a complete uproar over who should go first. We broke a piece of paper apart and drew sections for the shower order. I decided to forgo the order and just took a cold shower. I didn't want to wait and I didn't really care after living in my apartment in Santiago, where I went a couple of months without a hot (or even lukewarm) shower.

We drove a lot that day. I saw more pink radiating flamingos situated across the still blue waters of their lagoon. They were such a contrast to the monochromatic brown mountains. Where do flamingos come from anyway? Ever since I was a kid at the zoo and saw flamingos standing on one leg, I had always thought they were only a tropical bird and surely not from the frigid Altiplano of Bolivia. Everyone agreed they'd thought the same. What we didn't know then was that flamingos derive their bright color from the algae-rich contents of their environment; specifically a diet high in beta carotene found in algae that live in the Altiplano's lagoons. Looking back this left me a little confused, as the lagoons we passed were either bright green, pale blue, faded brown, or intense red.

Later that day we stopped in an Andean ghost town. There was a water tower that had what was probably a small leak trickling down, but the stream had frozen and subsequent leaking water had dripped down and frozen into an overflow of ice a few feet wide and five times as tall. The town was crumbling. Its industrial ruins were fading back into the salty organic roots of the Altiplano. Edgar said a train used to come twice a day and now only once every two weeks. Since the conditions were too harsh to grow food or raise animals, the remaining residents relied on the train supplies for their sustenance. Nothing surrounded that place except for dust and salt. Now only ten families lived among the crumbling wreckage of a once-prosperous town built on mineral wealth from salt and borax.

We found the few kids who were in town playing by us, hoping for some form of cross-cultural connection or gifting. One child had a sweater with all the NBA team logos on it, another a Disney hat. Both items were gray with dust and tearing at the seams. The South African photographer in our party passed out some of his extra chocolates to the children. After that one gesture everyone retreated back into the car as we waited for our driver to emerge from whichever hut he'd disappeared into. We suspected he'd been in conjugal bliss with one of the town's residents. I, however, hopped out of the car much to the surprise of my travel mates and tried to teach the children some numbers and words in English. We used the dirt covered side of the SUV to paint negative images of words in the absence of dust wherever my finger fell. I showed them that seco meant dry. This SUV was dusty and dry. They understood.

My fellow Gringos had reasons to refrain from interacting with the children (namely the wind, and possibly the dirtiness of these kids) but maybe it was my idea of getting the most out of this trip that made me exit the car. I just wanted to show these kids what we Americans were about. The children looked so interested and no one else was making an effort to break through the safe barrier of the Toyota Land Cruiser's steel doors. I could relate to everyone's fatigue but thought, let's knock down the walls and break barriers! Step 1: Show the children how to do a hand slap and fist pound greeting. In Estados Unidos this is how we do it! I thought that they'd take more away from a hand slap and fist pound than I would, but I might be kidding myself with that notion. I really treasure those memories! The whole situation, to me, was a microcosm of the type of charitable giving those far removed from the disadvantaged face. Just give them money, just give them chocolate bars, and then return to your comfortable life, your comfortable Toyota Land Cruiser, out of the coarse dust of reality that's hitting your eyes. Those that are better off are sometimes in that classification because they take steps to ensure their comfort, their advantage. But as I looked at everyone in the car and then back to the children in front of me I realized that these kids had something I, nor my fellow travelers in the car, would ever have again: innocence. They definitely had problems here but were essentially blinded to the world around them; blinded by the same dust that made their situation so bad. My Gringo friends and I, on the other hand, had all that we needed and then some. We were attuned to the issues of the less fortunate but lacked the capability to bridge the gap beyond anything more than a far-removed monetary gesture. I'll never forget how that tiny ghost town helped me to realize that problems need to be addressed head on, face-to-face, eye-to-eye in the dust that clouds our vision.

    We headed across the Salar de Uyuni, the largest salt flat in the world - said to encompass more than 10,000 square kilometers and contain more than 10 billion tons of salt. I expected that we would ride over miles of large salt granules and that it would be a very noisy ride as the SUVs tires treaded over the breakable mineral. Instead we followed a darkened path that petered off into the horizon. The path must've been a result of the exhaust and tire rubber wear-off from previous groups like ours. It was a pity to have taken part in leaving these tracks, but I reminded myself that at least the tour guides kept on the same path instead of creating a maze of tire tracks criss-crossing the salt. There were other reasons for staying on a consistent route. Edgar had told us that a few weeks before there was a crash between two SUVs. Something like nine tourists had died as well as the two drivers. I'd heard of the rampant drinking by the tour guides and was glad that our driver did not partake. But how could this happen? In a desert as big as Uyuni how hard could it be to avoid a crash when all you see is white around you? Wouldn't a black SUV coming toward you be noticeable? Clearly I wasn't hearing the entire story and never did.

    We were only a few miles into the salt desert and already I needed to urinate. I think the salt was dehydrating me just by looking at it. We pulled over by a small salt mining operation. Salt bricks were lying around that had been dug up. They reminded me of the snow bricks I had used to make the igloo many years before. Each was about the size of a shoe box. These large, white bricks reminded me of those I had cut many years before for the igloo I'd helped to make. They were even cut out of the solid ground in cookie-cutter fashion. My Irish friend and I looked around for a toilet. Our guide seemed to ignore our intentions as it was no doubt an offense to urinate on such a pristine geological formation. We found a stack of salt bricks and made our move.

Soon enough we were back in the car and caught sight of a giant hill rising out of the salt and coming up over the horizon. It was in fact an island. Strangely enough, no water surrounded the distant mound, but our guide assured us that it was still referred to as an island. This salt desert was an inland ocean many thousands of years ago. So what was initially an island would always be one.

Upon arrival, we found the island to be completely covered in cacti. After paying yet another entrance fee I had the chance to walk around and read a sign that many of these cacti were over 1,000 years old and grow nearly one centimeter per year. This island was used for sacred ceremonies by pre-Columbian peoples so the name of Incahuasi (Inca House in English) was fitting. I stood at the top and stared out over a sea of salt. It's said that in the rainy season, the salar is covered in water and that the light from the sky reflects to turn the white surface into a blue glow, rendering the surface and sky nearly indistinguishable from one another at the horizon.

From here we drove to a hostel comprised of salt and a couple of small souvenir shops that lined the outskirts of the desert. Salt had turned to dirt and dirt had turned to scrub bush. It was the end of the salar but the beginning of the Bolivian frontier. With all my travel experience Uyuni was the farthest from what I expected a tourist welcome for Bolivia to be, but in its destitution I discovered its sobering reality.

Photo 4: Incahuasi with the salt flat below.

❀ ❀ ❀

Butch Cassidy and the Sundance Kid, set in Bolivia and starring Robert Redford and Paul Newman, evokes images of a pristine subtropical land. They travel to Bolivia because it's rich in opportunity for exploitation and they are much too wanted by the U.S. authorities to keep swindling there. The villages portrayed in the movie have a distinct Southern Californian mix of oak trees and golden hills, and were obviously filmed less than a day's drive from the Hollywood studios. In fact, the town in which they decide to hold up a bank looks much like an old ghost town that may have been in the aforementioned actors' other movies. The set designers, however, managed to place some South American-looking pottery, some native-looking facades, and other trimmings like dustiness to ensure the town's authentic look. In actuality many Bolivian towns were developed by the non-indigenous European populations that arrived in Bolivia since the 16th century. Nevertheless the movie still reminds me of how Uyuni may have looked in it's earlier history; before it was completely exploited.

Our SUV arrived in Uyuni, and as we made our way from the salt flats to the city center I kept expecting the place to look like a city reputable of being named after the greatest salt flat on earth. But like the salt flats, it too was dead. The scattered slums gave way to dense shacks and these in turn gave way to crumbling brick buildings. Streets negatively formed, in the absence of the built environment. The garbage, animal or human waste and abandoned vehicles laid buried under a thin, sealing layer of dust. The air was stagnant. As the level of urbanity increased, the salt flats slipped out of view behind us. Strangely, the windiness present in he salt desert picked up into a light breeze. Newspapers, Coca-Cola bottles, and cigarette packs fluttered across the street like tumbleweeds must have done in years past when Butch and Sundance were laying low in a close by town.

    I grabbed my pack out of the SUV. It was heavy. We were two miles above sea level, but it was hot; a sticky hot. I wondered how much of this heat I could attribute to the actual weather, fearing any semblance of sweat was more due to my paranoia and utter shock than anything else. Uyuni was the first city I'd been to in Bolivia, though I had been in the country crossing the salar for two days. Technically we were here illegally. The first mission was for me and my fellow travelers to get immigration papers. Luckily the Irish guy in our group had a Lonely Planet Bolivia guide that included a map of Uyuni. The international police station was but a few blocks away. Arriving at the location we found a hostel in its place. The police station had never been there. The guide wasn't out of date – just completely wrong. This was but one of the many times I questioned the ground accuracy of the authors composing the book. I've worked on many projects in my cartography experience where matching a map to what actually existed on the ground was the most crucial step in the project. I assure you, it's not hard. These guys were just lazy. I felt the uncomfortable stares of the locals hit my cheekbones: I sure didn't want to miss the once-a-day bus and be stuck in this city for a night. We looked around for another hour and found the immigration office only to discover they were closed for an extended lunch.

Some of the SUV group had to catch a bus to La Paz, others to Potosi, and everyone needed money. We broke up and I went with my friend Sarah to buy a bus ticket to Potosi. It was easy, and 15 minutes later we circled back to the others who said they would have to wait and secure their spot in line for three hours until the ticket booth opened. I coughed. It was dusty. Even the dust was covered by a layer of dust. A few of us went to get food as it was two in the afternoon and no one had eaten all day. I first had to exchange money and my friend Carrie needed to find the one ATM before we could eat.

I went back and forth between the money exchangers and asked about their rates for exchanging Chilean pesos. I nervously gripped my wad of pesos, an excess of 200 American dollars. Never would I carry this much money with me but it was my leftover earnings from the teaching stint in Chile. I couldn't make deposits into any bank account so instead I managed to hide my money in my bag and amongst different clothing items so as to avoid a total loss in the event of a mugging. When I found an exchange rate that was only a partial rip-off I went ahead and removed the money from different spots, discretely, looking around calmly the whole time. Upon receiving the money, I recounted and re-diversified. We found Carrie's ATM, and I stood guard. She was pulling out more than me and would need it in La Paz. I was going to the jungle where things didn't cost much, but then again if I ran out of money or was mugged there would be no ATM to save me. I had to be aware of my surroundings and learn how to make do with minimal money.

We walked in and out of several small pizza shacks, all catering to the foreign traveler. Finally we found one where we thought we could save a buck. Sarah found us and sat down. A ten-year-old boy came out to take our order. The store was empty and dead – just like the town. I thought that since we were one of only two parties seated in the entire restaurant that we might get fast service. Our pizzas arrived about 70 minutes later. They were so cheap, but so, so good. My hunger was threefold at this altitude and the waxy cheese and starchy bread impeccably satisfied my palate.

It was finally time to get checked into the Republic so we made our way back to the international police office. Carrie and I (the two Americans) had to pay a $133 American dollar entrance fee for our visas while everyone else paid a nominal $10 administration fee. This law had been passed in several Latin American countries whose citizens were first charged the high entrance rate when they entered the U.S. So much for the golden rule. But I wasn't one of the lawmakers who wanted to make the Bolivians pay that much to get into my country. Hell, most couldn't even afford a plane ticket to the U.S., let alone a bus ride to the neighboring town. Generalizations aside, the issue of high American visa rates and pervasive poverty had more to do with U.S. lead IMF and World Bank policies than with the Bolivian people themselves. I was the one who should have felt guilty but after the international police threw in an additional $15 fee, because I didn't have proof of my vaccinations, I began to wonder if I'd be able to afford a bus trip out of Uyuni.

The others took off on their night bus for La Paz while Sarah and I walked around the town past dusk and waited for our departure. It was bitterly cold now, climatically, but my unfamiliarity and paranoia increased as night fell. Like the weather, my outlook became frigidly pessimistic. It was to be a six-hour bus ride to the highest city in the world, Potosi, which stood above 4,000 meters.

I thought that I'd better try and use the toilet because the bus didn't have one. If you've ever watched the movie *Trainspotting,* you know that in the first scene the guy goes into the most god-awful bathroom of some crummy pub in Scotland. That toilet pales in comparison with what I found at the bus terminal in Uyuni. But I thought it best to use this bathroom because it was the better alternative to, well, no bathroom. The old attendant sat there in her chair outside the stalls and handed me some tissue paper. Sarah and I took turns. For lack of better judgment I think I used the door labeled 'ducha', or shower? I was alerted to this after I opened the door to Sarah staring at me and asking, "Was that the shower?" It should be said that the necessary equipment was present but the attendant did give me a funny look.

We boarded the bus and I carried my pack with me. It was really too big to carry on and I hit several people in the face with the straps. I didn't want it stowed down below as I'd heard many stories about people catching a free ride in the luggage compartment and then going through the bags while down there. As a result, I had a quarter of the contents of my bag sitting on my lap and the other three quarters squeezed into any open portion of the narrow overhead storage. This didn't aid my effort in avoiding theft, though, as many of my items were openly displayed between peoples' belongings down the length of the bus. We took off for an overnight ride, lit dimly by the thin, waxing moon. At 6'3" and well above the height intended for use in the Japanese manufactured bus I couldn't move a limb. I floated in and out of consciousness, gripping my bag of personal effects, including my passport and money, dreaming of running with my legs free over a smooth (anything but bumpy) surface. Perhaps a flat beach. But Bolivia didn't have any ocean beaches. Chile took that land in war.

3. The Mountain that Eats Men

The bus arrived in Potosi at nearly one in the morning. The bus ride was seven hours long and we were given only one stop. My legs were restless and my back was sore. I grabbed a taxi ride from the first man who approached me with an offer. I thought I'd try to walk it or take a bus, but given the cheap rate he offered, the time of night, and the altitude, I thought it better to have someone who knew how to take me where I needed to go. I arrived to a tired doorman, signed in to the hostel, and immediately retired to bed.

I awoke the next day to the early morning sun and cold mountain air. I headed downstairs for a typical breakfast: bread rolls, butter, jam, and coffee. Over breakfast I heard other travelers commiserating over the appalling conditions of Potosi's infamous mine. I'd heard that one could tour the live mines but I knew nothing of the details. I saw, the night before, while checking in, that the hostel offered a booking service for the mine tour. I made my way to the front desk to sign and pay. The tour would leave in 30 minutes and so I rushed to lock up my things in a locker for the day. No time for a shower but I figured I wouldn't need it if I was going into a mine. With my best worse clothes on I was out the door with fellow hostelers.

    The tour agency was located in the back room of a row house. Our guide came in with a fresh hair cut, a mischievous-yet-enlightened smile, and his official tour guide badge slung over an orange jumpsuit. About a dozen of us were present and everyone was told to throw on a tattered yellow jumpsuit from a pile in the corner. We'd also need a pair of boots, a hard hat, and a head lamp unit. The dressed group passed through a small courtyard where a woman was washing some dishes in a small pail and we were led into the adjoining side street where a Japanese passenger van was waiting to pick us up. We made a brief stop to buy gifts for the miners. I thought I'd paid for my whole tour but, in typical tourism fashion, there was always an asterisk. See, I paid for the guide but would have to bring gifts for the miners in return for their graciousness in sharing the mine. With a bag of coca leaves, a pack of hand rolled cigarettes, and all the ingredients to make dynamite, I was set. Coca leaves were said to reduce altitude sickness and give energy. They were even used to reduce hunger pangs, which were frequent since the miners worked in the mines the whole day without food.

    The bus zigzagged up the switchbacks of the mountain that was said to be higher than 4 kilometers. The mountain named Cerro Rico, or rich hill in English, practically singlehandedly funded the expansion of the Spanish Empire. The folklore says that at one time there was enough silver extracted from Cerro Rico to make a silver bridge from Potosi to Spain, and that this bridge would be used to transport the rest of the silver from the mine back to Spain. But the wealth of this mine came with a cost. Our guide stated that from 1545 to 1825 it is estimated that eight million Black and Indian slaves died in mining operations! While the Indians were acclimated to the altitude and bitter cold, they were far fewer in number than the Africans. So many Black slaves were taken directly to Potosi but died shortly after their arrival because of the cold and thin air (among the slew of other factors associated with being a slave). In the past and, to this day, the mountain carries the nickname of "The Mountain That Eats Men".

    We passed ore carts that were now full of zinc rather that silver. We passed weathered and dust-covered men resting under the shade of a cave opening. The city was visible directly below the barren mountain. I wondered what kept this mountain standing; having been mined for 400 years it was probably just as barren on the inside as it was outside. The van came to a stop and we got out and crowded around our guide. We were standing next to a Spanish church that was said to be constructed shortly after the Spaniards discovered that the mountain contained precious metals. Apparently, if there was a church there, then the mountain was considered sacred and the Spaniards would be justified in seizing it from the indigenous peoples. But either way, the indigenous peoples had considered the mountain sacred far before their European conquerors. As a matter of fact, the Inca Empire took limited precious metal for ceremonies. The Inca were by no means the first to lay claim to Cerro Rico and took it from the Quechua descendants they conquered, who gave it the name Sumaj Orko.

Our guide took out a stick of dynamite, a fuse string, and a putty form of chemical reactant. A no-show of hands met his request for volunteers to help assemble the dynamite. Once again he asked, but this time with short jabs about courage, or rather the lack thereof. Still no hands. I was getting impatient and so I raised my hand and walked forward simultaneously. I stood in front of the crowd and put fuse to putty to stuffed dynamite stick. In one hand I held the stick and in the other the end of the fuse. Then the guide lit the end of the fuse. Wait! I didn't sign up for this. He explained the basic process of TNT, how it was used in the mines, and how twice a day the miners cleared the mines to set off their TNT. The first was in the early morning, the second in the early afternoon. We were in between the scheduled times and would have to light our own TNT if we wanted to see an explosion. How generous of this man, I thought, but I was still holding onto an ever-decreasing fuse. He took the TNT from me and gave everyone a closer look. I felt relieved as the fuse was ¾ of its size from a few minutes prior. But then he insisted that I hold it again. This time, in a playful manner, he laughed after a few awkward seconds and grabbed it back. He then looked at me and mumbled something about how the fuse was getting dangerously low. So he parted a path between our onlooking group and ran over to a side of the hill that was maybe 50 meters away. He ran back and told us all to have our cameras ready – there would be a big explosion. It's interesting, though, that when you're expecting something it takes so long to come. Finally, when even our guide had thought it to be a dud, we heard the explosion and felt our bodies shake. Any shrapnel had been blown away from us as the stick was positioned professionally by our guide. I caught the explosion just a few seconds too late due to the delay on my camera and, as a result, I got a great shot of a mound of dirt.

The cave entrance was discrete except for the blackish Rorschach blots that stained the rock lining. This was said to be dried llama blood from only a couple of days ago; the miners sacrifice a llama every week in hopes of bringing safety. We entered the mine from what was supposed to be the third level. After many generations of miners, though, I was unconvinced that even the most experienced, and living, miner would know where the tunnels began and ended. The tunnel began to follow some ore cart tracks, with caged lighting strung overhead. Puddles of what I could only imagine to be a mix of condensation and the most toxic of chemicals emerged between the shadows created by the ceiling light. We veered off to the left and down a set of ladders. I felt like I was in a giant game of Chutes and Ladders that I'd played as a child. I stayed close to our leader. My childhood urge to explore every passageway was abated when our guide would take what appeared to be a dead end, leaving me to place no question in my judgment of routes. Without our guide I was a regular Tom Sawyer, lost in the cave.

We stopped periodically to let the active miners pass. They carried tools though few preceded by with much loot. It was explained that the glory days of this mine were long gone. Instead, these miners relied on the occasional zinc deposit but really hoped to strike it rich some day with the elusive silver rumored to be hiding in the mountain, even after all these years. As a miner you could be expected to work about 15 years before succumbing to silicosis pneumonia. Their life expectancies were so much shorter because of the high level of immediate death in the mine and the possibility of slow deaths caused by lung problems. But these risks seemed small under the weight of silver-lined dreams.

One miner I passed was doing nothing more than lowering a bucket down a shaft to his partner. He probably wasn't older than 30 but looked weathered and dusty. I smiled to him though he returned no such grace to me. What was I really doing to help him? Probably just getting in his way and making him hate his lot in life that much more. So I gave him my dynamite supplies and the cigarettes, wrapped up in a plastic bag. His gratefully accepted it with nothing more than a nod.

Our party continued on until we reached an alcove at the end of a corridor. We were stopped by our guide and he prefaced us about the contents that lay within. There was a god figure inside the room. This was indeed a shrine that lay within the heart of the mountain. So far removed from fresh air, so far removed from the heights of heaven, and so far removed from any setting that would evoke images of monks worshiping in their pristine surroundings. We entered the small room and crowded around its walls. There were clay benches to sit on; any negative space now filled by our bodies was surely blasted out of the mountain's interior to create the mounds of rock on which I was resting my weight. In the middle of us was a seated clay figure, attentively sitting erect as if he was on a throne. He had horns, a dog-like nose, clear translucent eyes and large protruding arms with fingernails on his hands that were made from human donations. His head was covered in coca leaves, as was most of his torso, less his crotch where a giant clay penis stood erect. Long colored strings hung from his ears. In his hand he held cigarettes and on his lap rested a small bottle of grain alcohol. His name was Tios. There were a few such alcoves like this throughout the mountain and, once a week, the workers would gather at their local shrine and give thanks to Tios in hope of a good find that week. They would smoke cigarettes with him, adorn him in coca leaves, and sip on grain alcohol in his presence. They had the llama and the Tios; kill the living so that you shall live, drink with the dead so that you may reap rewards before you pass beyond carnal existence.

So as the miners did, we did. I shared a cigarette with an Irish guy. No regular cigarette — a fat hand-rolled cigarette that looked more like a cigar. At about two and a half miles above sea level and within the depths of an air deprived cave, this was no easy task. I was dizzy and could barely breathe. But I would find silver! Then came the bottle of grain alcohol from our guide. I took a swig as I wondered what the badge of accreditation around his neck really entailed. We took a few minutes of silence and

I imagined all the slaves that had passed through here, even this particular cave and seat where I sat. These slaves might have been desperate enough to turn from their native religions and embrace this underworld god. A couple of days down here on the brink of death would surely change many people's opinions about religion. The difference was that these slaves wouldn't see any of the rewards for the silver they mined.

We made our way out of the mine via ore cart tracks in a lighted tunnel, much like how we entered, but this time we were on the second story of the tunnels.. The sunlight was more intense than I ever imagined. My eyes had adjusted to the thin glow of lamps for the past two hours. Just as the sun emerged, so did the tourist trap that was waiting for us. Two young boys carried around a collection of different types of rocks and minerals. They begged for us to buy an assorted bag. The multiple points of sale throughout the tour seemed to have more layers than the mine itself. Neither my backpack nor my bank account had room for the fantastic, and surely well earned, collection of minerals. We got in the car and headed down the hill to change out of our muddy clothes. When I was ready to leave, an announcement was made that tips were surely welcome. I was beginning to expect that. I thanked our guide and continued onward. I was centavo-less and a verbal gesture would have to do.

While in Potosi I managed to see the old Spanish minting press which was now a museum. This particular building used to produce the silver coinage for the whole Spanish empire. Donkeys would work around the clock, walking in circles to drive the gears needed for pressing. But now the mint was out of use. Bolivia no longer makes its coins but instead outsources currency production to France. I spent the rest of my time in Potosi walking the streets past beggars and hangers-on. Why is it that the people so close to wealth see none of its rewards?

Photo 5: 'Tios' is Quechua for 'Dios' (God in Spanish). Quechua speakers don't use the letter D in their alphabet. Tio is the god of the underworld.

On my last day in Potosi I met a Scottish guy traveling to Sucre. My interest was peaked when I found out that he was going back to Scotland for a job as a railway transportation planner He and I took the morning coach to one of Bolivia's two capital cities. This was also on my way toward the farm that I'd soon be living on. I'd always had a desire to labor for my own sustenance and learn methods of self reliance. Particularly I was interested in how one might survive off the grid with the rising costs and virtual end of oil based food and commercial production. During the daytime bus ride I fell in and out of a napping state but the intermittent light afforded me an opportunity to see the vegetation change as the bus slowly descended to a lower elevation.

◎ ◎ ◎

The Scot and I arrived in Sucre, a town that gave off a Mediterranean feel with its white-washed buildings and red tiled roofs. The change in weather towards a hot afternoon also may have contributed to my feeling of displacement. Still, we got off the bus to a well-maintained terminal and no homeless or destitute population. Immediately we hailed a taxi to take us to the hostel that we'd picked out in my travel companion's guide book. Weighed down by our bags we searched the block up and down a few times only to find that what was supposed to be a hostel was instead a blank door. I guess they'd packed up shop in the last year since the book had been published. My illusion of a Mediterranean paradise was once again fed when two well-dressed young European women stood in front of the door where our hostel should have been. I explained our predicament and they had no clue where the hostel could have gone. Instead they offered to take us to the hostel where they were staying. This seemed nice and I happily obliged. On the way there, they went into detail with their high-class British accents about how the hostels in Sucre were grimy and gross. My only motive was to save my ever-shrinking pocket full of money. Upon arriving at their hostel, through the coded gate and locked terrace, things became clearer. It was more of a bed and breakfast than anything else. It could have been fun, but our minds were quickly made up when we heard the only room left had just one bed. That would be a little too friendly. So the Scot and I found a low budget extended stay motel down the street, complete with screaming Bolivian kids.

It was Friends Day in Bolivia and so we walked around that afternoon hoping to befriend or be befriended. We came across two more girls – one from England and the other from California. They, too, were dressed more affluently than the typical traveler. I met these girls whilst looking at some Alpaca blankets to buy and after a few common threads were established with the U.K. and Cali connections, we decided to get some dinner and beers at the local Gringo bar. It felt just like home with the $12 Tex Mex plate and $4 beers. The spending spree continued into the night when we visited a Dutch restaurant that had been promoted to us earlier and then went for a night cap at a hookah bar. It was a friendly day and I was glad to have met some friends who liked to spend money as much as me.

I woke up the next morning with a slightly lighter fanny pack and decided I would leave immediately. Upon checking with the bus company I found out it was a 16 hour bus ride to get to the farm with the bus leaving at five or six in the evening. So I spent the day visiting the Judicial museum which seemed fitting as Sucre is Bolivia's judicial capital. Power had been decentralized in an effort to unify the country and prevent dictatorship. If the museum taught me one thing it's that this plan never really worked. The facility was an effigy to wars past. Most of these wars resulted with Bolivia ceding land to the victor. The drab walls made me long for living history.

Fittingly I exited the museum to a screaming crowd. Old women were being pushed away from the gates of a ministerial building by federal police. I couldn't figure out the direct cause but surely the IMF or some distant neoliberal policy dressed up as 'international aid' was indirectly to blame. I headed over to an Internet café so that I could talk with family before I disappeared into the woods, and off the grid, for a couple of weeks. As I talked with my sister on the phone I could hear gun shots from the protesters outside. These were fired skyward to bring people out to the streets. I thought nothing of it though it was much different than anything that was going on at the other end of the line.

I made it to the bus terminal and bought the series of tickets necessary to get me first into the terminal and then onto the bus. I waited around to check my bag under the bus for nearly an hour, all the while carrying my pack on my back. I was determined not to lose anything through thievery or personal ineptitude right before I left civilization. My pants hung down below the line created by my pack's tightened belt strap. I saw people looking at me but disregarded it. When I finally found the porter he just laughed at me. My low-hanging pants were reason enough to identify me as American though I was sure the porter had never been to Oakland. I tried to get a ticket receipt but he just kept laughing along with a handful of bus patrons who'd caught on. In my defense, these were the jeans I bought in Chile. They were the equivalent of ten bucks. Sure, they were almost falling off, but they did the job, and for cheap!

I boarded the bus and got a seat next to a Bolivian kid of, maybe, 14. On the other side of me was some French girl, probably in her mid-twenties. The boy didn't want to talk after I mentioned I was coming from Chile. He must have either hated me for being affiliated with Chile, as most people in his country did, or only spoke Quechua. I'd like to think the latter. The French girl loved to talk. She was wearing a fedora. I hate fedoras. The whole style emerged as a female fashion trend and was made big when men started to wear the hats during the 1920's. It seems unoriginal unless, of course, you're a Prohibition Era gangster. I enjoyed stretching out my legs in the aisle and got ready for the big descent into the eastern lowlands. Though by the time the bus got out of the city, the entire aisle had been taken up by squatters. They would take the bus for free and lay on the ground for the night. The ticket clerk hopped over squatters by balancing his feet on seat arm rests as he collected ticket stubs. I fell in and out of consciousness with the Bolivian kid on my right shoulder and the squatter lady clinching on to my left-hand arm rest as we careened through the mountain road in the middle of the night.

4. Ginger's Paradise

They're balancing on a coffee tree branch. The beans they pick will be dried for coffee and the shells soaked to make a tea. Here, nothing is wasted. Strong coffee-tea is what they'll need when up before sun, milking the cow. Some days they may chop wood and find a freshly-laid egg in the wood pile, other days they'll use the wood to fuel a fire and boil those eggs. On the farm travelers and locals collaborate in learning how to harvest, learning how to heal, and learning how to forget the outside world. They come down to the cabin at night for the quinoa chocolate and leave questioning their chess skills, care of the dreadlocked chess master who runs the farm and cultural inn.

The following journal entries describe the time I spent on an organic and sustainable farm in Bermejo, Bolivia. Initially, I thought I would stay for over a month but my stay ended up lasting for ten days. My financial situation had changed so I had to shorten the time it would take to make it to Ecuador where my return flight to the U.S. Was already scheduled. Although I believe there is something to be said about staying a while in one place in order to gain a full understanding of life within that sphere, I realized that there were other locales I wanted to see in a finite amount of time. I feel that within ten days I was able to gain a small understanding of farm life in a rural valley through hard work, a hard bed, no dinners, and the absence of commercial products and other outside influences, such as news. The ten consecutive days represent a fastidious journal-keeping effort. I wrote almost daily, sometimes writing in the morning and evening. It is through the medium of journal writing that I hope to convey to the reader the fullest sense of my experience.

July 25th, 2008

After an overnight bus with babies crying and women sleeping in the aisles, not to mention a Bolivian guy sleeping on my shoulders, I am finally here at Ginger's Paradise...

I arrived when the sun was just breaking through the mist. A true cloud forest. Beautiful: hens, dogs and native people who sustain themselves on farming... rambling through the different types of trees.

I've started work on a water-catchment/water-power canal by digging a ditch and slashing through brush with a machete. There's a guy from Switzerland and one from Israel. The owners Sol and Cristobal are welcoming. Cristobal went to California Polytechnic University. My brother Eric would laugh if he knew someone from Cal

Poly became this hippie with dreads. Cristobal said he hasn't been back to the U.S.A. in 16 years. I sense how distant he is to common events that seem only five months in the past for me. He seems *happy* though.

Photo 6: *Ginger's Paradise sign at the Sucre-Santa Cruz road.*

July 26th, 2008

Just went to a Bolivian high school beauty pageant. Backstreet Boys and Grease were playing to some dance moves. Not too much different than my homecoming. This was for the national 'Dia de Amistad' (Friendship Day). I arrived with the two sons of the couple who own the farm where I'm staying. Nova is in the 6th grade and is a remarkable translator, and Dizzy is in 4th grade. I can see how they look up to me. The amount of questions they ask makes me realize how hard fatherhood would be should I ever choose that path. I picked some coffee beans today and slashed a hornets' nest in half with a machete...tomorrow is Sunday and will be chill...I'd like to bake a meal from and for the farm one of these days.

July 27th, 2008

Went to the swimming hole. Will write more tomorrow!

July 28th, 2008

Well, waking up early this morning to help milk the cow, after a first day of resting, a solid day [of work], and Sunday off. I have decided to make a renewed effort. I'm going to try to live here as cheaply as possible (hopefully free) and work hard for a couple of weeks, though I hope I can learn something more than digging a ditch. I think moving into the worker cabin, from my present location at the guest house, with Beet will help as I'll be closer to the cow and other WWOOF (World Wide Opportunities on Organic Farms)/servant duties. My goal was three weeks.

I've changed it to two...I need to stick to two...I'm not going to count on any girl I meet to fulfill my other week or two on a farm in Ecuador...this is my experience...and I need to milk it.

Beet is a surprisingly interesting guy, probably about 20, from Switzerland, and is going to university for a geography degree after traveling. We had some good talks over beers last night and it serves to reconfirm that 20-something is an age of curiosity, drive and passion that I would like to teach. He tells me how he wants to move back to Zürich to be with his friends, ride his city bike, and go to university. Why would it be so bad to settle down in a place with people I know and like for a while? Maybe even go back to school to teach? (University of Oregon has a good program although I'd have to move to Portland to gain residency). Why couldn't I get back into UW for the teaching program? Why did this never hit me? Hmmm...wow!! I could probably create my own teaching track if need be...lots to consider. One thing is for sure though: don't think I want this type of farming-retreat-getting-away-from-it lifestyle. Sure, it's great getting back to the land, teaching and showing people how you live, and exposing them to country living as is being done to me or even pursuing a life closer to nature. BUT to me it seems like giving up on society. I am a product of society. I need it as much as it needs me. No I take that back; it needs me more. I have so much to offer society, so much to offer its people, its problems, its kids, its adults, its culture. I can make a bigger difference inside the machine rather than out. I have to find my creative niche to make it work and a career has to have the capacity to be continually changing and evolving. Many people have told me I should be a teacher, even shaman. Why the hell would I want to gain knowledge from psychoactives for a purpose in life? That's the lazy, and in my family, disrespected approach. A healer? Well maybe, but I'd rather learn and change rather than absorb peoples' problems. I would now call myself spiritual. But a guru type healer? Now that's never what I dreamed about being as a child. I dreamed about being a paleontologist, an astronaut, in short an explorer...a discoverer of new ideas. And what do discoverers want to find? Maybe riches, but also they want to advance and change other ideas and preconceptions about strongly held beliefs. This is what I'm doing every day with issues on the environment, on peak oil sustainability, geographical perspectives on old and new subjects.

We (Beet, the two boys and myself) went to the swimming hole yesterday. What I imagined as a serene, tranquil, pure and natural setting had a hotel situated on the bank of the lagoon, man-made terraces, a golf course and meadows. There were beautiful meadows otherwise clear-cut to make way for the unnatural fertilized roll-out grass. It brings me back to a childhood book about how a five-star hotel was erected on Everest and a McDonald's at the Grand Canyon: the future that is now likely and that I must now stop. I can show others how to prevent it from happening while still maintaining my own goals to the same end. With teaching I have the time and capacity for this. Anything is possible when you set your mind to it. *My mind is set.*

July 29th, 2008

How many days does this month have? Today will be my fifth day on the farm. Farm life is tough and I've been sleeping ten hours the last couple of nights. I macheted a berm and carried 6" PVC pipes all day. I am sore and should probably do some yoga. I should probably do only a little though. I get to cook all day today so that will be a much needed break for "Superhero Jeff" as Chris (Cristobal) calls me. I am so glad I'm doing this on my own. Looking back on my entire trip, I have done things, taken advantage of every invite and every opportunity. I hope to even do the horse trek to the 'old way of living' villages and to Che's starting point. I'm not simply reading, I'm living, doing, and actualizing my dreams and desires. I knew a girl that would always tell me she was the kind of person that did things while I was the kind of person who just read about them. I don't know what she's talking about. Today I bathed in the river while looking at the cloud forest and couple thousand foot cliffs in the distance. I kept repeating 'Living in Bolivia' over and over in my head to James Brown's "Living in America" beat.

All I've been thinking about is moving back to Seattle to start anew in a city I know and love. Time will tell me if its right but I just wish time would hurry up so I could start *testing time*. I'm excited to go there with the mentality I have now and will be sure to have when I'm done with this trip.

July 31st, 2008

It's my seventh day, Beet's last. He's been here 13 days. I don't know if I'll stick it out that long. I'm longing for friends, new places, and maybe a little romance. When I do solitary work my mind always reverts to calculating the monetary feasibility of my trip, always trying to rationalize why I'm here doing manual labor and really not sure if I'm paying for food and lodging here. I'm sleeping a lot mainly due to exhaustion, covered in insect bites. My arms and feet look like a polka dot print dress from sand fly bites, and my body is sore. Worst of all I'm not devoting the free time I have to learning Spanish or seriously writing. I keep thinking about being on the beaches of Northern Peru, in the sun with a drink and some ceviche, maybe even trying some surfing. I hear it's cheap living there too.

Yesterday I carried wood in a wheelbarrow, peeled some other wood for furniture, and perhaps the only fun activity was making fliers for this place which meant I got to do a little drawing. The redeeming part is that I was complimented on it. The day before, I had the pleasure of cooking burritos. I made the tortillas from scratch and cooked up some salsa as well. Later that day I used a wheelbarrow to carry sugar across the river, held a parrot, pushed a Ford truck with five Bolivians, and pushed a wheelbarrow full of some concrete across a questionably hanging suspension bridge. Realistically I'll give myself a few more days here. I find it funny how I/everyone always wants what they can't have. I keep mentioning how I could really go for some Oreos or a Dairy Queen Peanut Buster Parfait, much to Cristobal's chagrin. He's been here long enough where he can filter that out but I am still in summer camp mode, knowing that there is an end to this lifestyle in sight. I even want Coca-Cola! And I want to cut my hair, I want to meet a nice girl to cut it, I want to meet a nice girl who will bike the 'Road of Death' with me, walk up to Machu Pichu on the train tracks and travel for a while. I came here wanting to learn things and now I'm here and realizing these are self-taught skills I can teach myself and this is just for the hands-on experience. Am I doing it for myself or to prove (to the world, my family, a girl, friends) that, yes I had the fortitude to stick it out for 'X' weeks? I came here in the first place, have realized it's different, have experienced that realization, and that counts for a lot. Perhaps I should humble myself and suck it up, leave early if *I* feel like it.

It was interesting to hear Cristobal, who I thought was your prototypical hippie, go on about how selfishness was the key. His example came from the "Fountainhead" by Ayn Rand. She supposes that if you are selfish then you will drive things to your ends. If these ends are to help, better, and relieve people then it is better to be selfish to see these ends out. But if you are always being philanthropic or compromising your ideals with others then you never invest enough in yourself to achieve your aims. This is what I would expect to hear from an anarchist, which he is, having abandoned society. He lets people come to him now. Funny though, how he still relies on society to make his living. I believe he is a product of a step-by-step process of letting things flow and fall into place. To a degree, his selfishness led him to remove himself from society, where he now watches things unfold by his own accord. I need to move ahead in my own selfish manner. I need to stop watching things happen. Dad was right: "Some people get it and some people don't."

August 1st, 2008

Well, Beet's gone and I moved into the volunteer shack, as I was alerted of my full WWOOF status yesterday. From here on out it's free living, minus my indentured servitude clause (like moving firewood, for example).

I found a book on Peruvian civilizations and might take it with me when I leave. I have been dreaming about Seattle, my friends, UW football games, and the autumn air. I decide I will leave the farm Wed or Thursday morning, which will be about two weeks and this will give me enough time to get to La Paz for the weekend. I need some "Big City Nights" after this experience!!! ...I wanna climb the 'Portal del Diablo' on Sunday. I need snacks for that to work. Perhaps I will go into town today after lunch.

It's the afternoon now and I'm amazed how fast my plans have changed. I no longer wanna climb the 'Portal del Diablo' but would rather put my energy into leaving here on Monday morning. If I have a free day Sunday then that's fine but I found out about a festival, a fish festival, happening in a few days and am excited to go to a small town (with maybe a few Gringos) where I can listen to traditional music and watch dance or participate if I drink enough. I decided, today after hearing what Sol said about traveling, that I don't want to pay for a trek up to Machu Picchu. It seems like the real rewards of traveling lay along the path you create for yourself rather than a path which someone leads you on. Perhaps and *only* perhaps will I even hike the train tracks.

I would find more gratitude if I consciously chose not to go to Machu Picchu because it is so run-over and unsustainable. Could it really be enjoyable to go up there with a train load of tourists? 'Oh but it's *just* one day, oh well you'll *only* see it once in your life. If I can foot it up there, at least it will be an adventure and more sustainable. Why not, instead, go to more small cities, like Villa Tunari, with the fish festival? Besides there are so many things I haven't heard about and will want to do. I can do ten of these things for the price of Machu Picchu, with ten different places, ten different people and ten different perspectives on what is sustainable tourism. Similarly, I have decided to end my farm stay with ten days experience. I feel this is a good compromise. I have committed for a long time, I've grown accustomed to the trials and hardships of farm/rural living, and experienced something similar to what my ancestors must have gone through in Nebraska, Ireland, or otherwise. I have craved dinner, I have craved Coke, Oreos, women, itch-less skin, and a few other necessities I thought I could have lived without. Even a haircut and shave will not come soon enough. It's funny how you always want what you can't have and right now I would love some pumpkin pie...cchhha wait I will eat some tonight or tomorrow!!! Fresco!! In the meantime, Cristobal and Sol with their children have been open, welcoming and instructive with me.

Photo 7: Obi-wan Kenobi's cabin in the cloud forest.

It's evening now and I'm in my bunk. My experience here is different from what I expected. I envisioned more merriment in the garden, things going with ease, a catered farm experience to the eco-tourist (myself). This has not been the reality and, like Santiago, was difficult for me when trying to get the smallest thing done; this has been the same to the nth degree. Although

Ginger's Paradise relies on the financial support of outsiders (tourists and WWOOFers) and buys minimal things like sugar and pasta, they are good with the amount of products/essentials they take off the land to sustain themselves and I feel like they are becoming more independent. They milk their cow daily, make their own coffee, 90% of their food, etc.

As I sit here in Obi-Wan Kenobi's cabin (what everyone calls the WWOOF shack because a hermit use to live there before Cristobal acquired it) and listen to the ever-growing current of the cloud-forest-sourced river in my proximity, I recall the movie on which I had based most of my adolescent beliefs: SLC Punk. I remember the pretext being 'never sell out' and the outcome 'You gotta buy in to something eventually.' Cristobal here at the farm has told me about his punk days; recalling the length of his Mohawk with pride and a certain glow. (I guess he was too punk to listen to NOFX teaching us that 'He's more punk than me' gets old fast). Well, Chris was more punk than me, wearing his American flag and nothing else on stage. He didn't sell out then and he certainly hasn't sold out now with his beliefs. Much respect for a man who can live off the grid on his own construction, will, and hard work. He certainly isn't hurting anybody and he's actually creating an instructional venue for others to see the possibilities of independent, sustainable living. But he's sold out in my book. Removing yourself this much from society isn't punk. In the words of an Anti-Flag concert I once attended, "being the best you can be at something, that's what punk is to me." Put it all together and for him maybe this is the best. I hope it is and it certainly seems like he enjoys it. But I wanna affect more, I wanna teeter on the edge of 'the system' looking in just long enough to change it and then step out for a bit of fresh air and a little light. By moving out to a retreat like Ginger's Paradise I don't feel like I can give back nearly as much as being inside this crazy world. As I told Cristobal, "Great thinkers are people who can hold two opposing ideas in their mind at one time while juxtaposing them against one another." If you're on either side of the seesaw, then how are you going to know what it's like when you're down, and down when you're up? The only way to go is by teetering in the middle with a foot firmly placed on either side and with as wide of a stance as possible.

August 4th, 2008

I woke up this morning at five and caught the first bus to Santa Cruz. It was *packed* the whole two hours. I'm glad. I'm glad not to have stayed/visited this city. From everything I see it's a complete mess. Uyuni incarnate. Right now I'm munching away on the starchiest bread I've ever eaten. I'm on my way to Villa Tunari and after ten minutes our bus got a flat tire. On the plus side, I think the road may be paved the whole way.

I met a couple from Breckenridge, Colorado and along with Dizzy, Nova and Gaia the farm dog, we ascended a mudslide laden hill. I felt like a 12 year old again; blazing trails and then taking a polar bear swim in the river afterwards to wash off all the red clay that covered my skin. The Coloradoans recommended a great monkey/puma refuge to me which I plan on going to upon my arrival in Villa Tunari.

I can tell Nova looks up to me with all I know. We talked about quantum physics for a few minutes while making sugar. I told Nova that there was a public television science show in the United States which is named after him, *Nova*. His eyes lit up because he's fascinated by science. I left on good and thankful terms with everyone. Hugs ensued; I hit the sack after a couple of good chess losses. I really hope Nova breaks out of that small town and does something great. It seems hard to be the oldest kid on the family farm. A lot to live up to while still 12. I can only inspire...

5. Spider Monkeys and Pejerreyes

Revelations: 1) On Bolivian buses, people defecate in a hole right next to the driver. 2) No matter how dumb I think I look, I should know I already look dumb and just ask for directions before I walk around with a 60-lb pack for 45 minutes. 3) Clothes-washing facilities does not mean washer and dryer; it means with your hands and a bar of soap. 4) Bottled Coca-Cola tastes a lot different in Bolivia. I was expecting to be satiated by familiar corn-syrup. I did feel the caffeine or something like it but wondered what's really in the name *Coca*-Cola for the Bolivian market?

As I was getting off the bus in Villa Tunari I passed by a man who was defecating next to the bus driver, with a clear stench and audibly apparent flatus. So this was why I'd seen so many people descend the stairs to the lower level of the bus. And this was why we hadn't taken any pit stops, which I'd found to be a regular occurrence on other

Bolivian buses, even if it was for the bushes. Without a pony wall or barrier to surround his naked torso my eyes veered up and met his for an uncomfortable half second: me with a look of puzzlement and him with a stare of guiltless complacency as if to say, 'Hey man, this is how it is – when you gotta go, you gotta go.'

I was glad to exit my last form of transportation for the day. I had not imagined this end to what turned out to be a 13 hour, multiple connection route. I'd been up since 4:30 in the morning, when I left the farm to catch the first 'flota', or mini bus, to Santa Cruz. The morning's flota was overcrowded, forcing me to sit sideways on the floor. The flota curved back and forth along the gravel road in the black of the early morning, stopping occasionally for another roadside guest to squeeze in, on and over.

Upon making it to the bus terminal in Santa Cruz, I looked for a free seat on a larger and bathroom-equipped bus bound for Cochabamba that could drop me off in Villa Tunari, about halfway to the bus' destination. Though the bus was advertised as toilet-equipped, I never suspected as I entered the doorway that the wooden seat next to the driver lifted up. Nevertheless, I managed to secure the front seat on the top deck of the bus which allowed me to view the open road ahead with an unobstructed view almost as if I were soaring like the Andean condors that inhabited this region. The panoramic view gave me a clear insight into the vastness of what was dubbed "Coca Country" by the Clinton administration in years past. I frequently saw soldiers of the Bolivian Army pass in the back of untagged pick up trucks, holding on to their two meter long wooden staffs. The few things more frequent on this stretch of the highway were the mandarin sellers that invaded the bus at every government checkpoint, and flags declaring each pueblo's political alliance. The colors of the flags, which were based on agricultural and land ownership rights, changed often as the bus meandered across the fluid border between eastern and western Bolivia.

The fight for land ownership had gone on in this region for several decades as a result of IMF imposed regulations on coca production. Coca farmers were historically banned from growing their product that is steeped in the Bolivian diet and culture. The ban didn't even differentiate between sustenance farming and for profit coca production which led many to flee the region or fight the power, the latter of which was never successful when CIA operatives had no accountability except tons of coca seized. With every new U.S. led foreign aid package would come a stipulation for lowering the coca production and the necessity for the government to clear farmers from their land, indiscriminately, in order to achieve a reportable statistic for the war on drugs. This method, though, is hopefully relegated to the past. Since Evo Morales, a former coca grower, has taken office aid packages have been declined and growers have been given small allotments big enough for diversified planting capable of sustaining a family. Now the question of land ownership has more to do with taking land from foreign resource extraction companies, who drill for oil and gas, and nationalizing the rights and profits to benefit a larger segment of the population.

Several hours passed and I was dropped off on the side of a road that looked like a stylized American western ghost town. Lining the road were decrepit buildings, dusty streets, and old motels that weren't clearly open or closed. Yet the town was current in its commercial offerings: storefronts hung beach towels adorned with super heroes, pizza shacks existed in the buildings that weren't selling towels, and the motels had names like 'Las Palmas'; all of which evoked a sense of sentimentality for my native California. I couldn't truly tell if I was in the heart of Bolivia or on the sun-soaked west coast of the United States. Then my answer came as my eyes began to focus on the immediate surroundings. A white guy, twenty-something, walked on by with baggy pants, skate shoes, and scruffy hair. Okay, easy mix-up, surely just another traveler. I set on my way to find a hostel for the night and soon I walked by another fair-skinned dude my own age. He was playing a game called diabolo, which uses a pair of wooden sticks connected by a string to spin a yo-yo like double disc. He spun the disc back and forth, catching it behind his back and spinning it under his legs. The dude had dreads.

The bus had gone too far and I was already back in California. I still hadn't seen any of Peru or Ecuador. This was wholly unfair. Upon finding my hostel I let my pack slip off my chaffed shoulders, knowing that I would need to look into the contents later that night to see what could be thrown away in order to diminish its weight. I immediately asked if there was an available room, in English, for I was tired, confused, and felt like I was probably back in the States. "No entiendo, habla en español, por favor." A Spanish response could very well mean I was in Southern California, and I proceeded to ask her in Spanish if she had an available room. She responded with a derisive "Si", and proceeded to a room to put my stuff down. In the quarters I looked out the window, and watched as a Bolivian soldier got out of his car.

Upon realizing that I was indeed in Villa Tunari, Bolivia, I felt certain that I should rethink my game plan. Currently I looked like I belonged in California. I'd developed a beard fitting for any Sierra Nevada mountain man and the hair on top of my head hadn't been cut since I left the States nearly five months prior. It seemed like any free time over the preceding five month span had gone to twisting and knotting my hair in an effort to become dreaded. Currently, though, my auburn-brown locks were a mix of dreads, knots, curls (which I didn't know I was capable growing) and surely some living organisms. After all, it's common knowledge that coroners found 42 species of previously undiscovered bugs in Bob Marley's hair after he died. This final ingredient in the ever-thickening quaff was what led me to grab my scissors, my soap, and a stubby razor. I went to the shared bathroom at the end of the hall and locked myself in for an hour and a half. What followed was a very uneven hair cut, though I had no complaints seeing as how this had been my first attempt at self-cutting.

I would later secretly hope to continue this burgeoning skill, but when I arrived back in the U.S. I grew too fond of the flirtatious Asian hairstylists at Supercuts to keep up on the self-maintenance. A family joke circulated about the time my Dad had stretched as his hairstylist took off his smock, and he accidentally brushed his hand against her. The hairstylist responded with, "Ewe knotee boi," in a southeast Asian accent. The attitude was well worth the cost.

With my top hair sporadically trimmed and my bangs short enough to be mistaken for Jim Carrey's character in *Dumb and Dumber*, I headed out to find an Internet-ready computer in order to inform friends and relatives of my successful emergence from the farm and jungle.

My stomach craved dinner, anything for dinner, since this third meal was not provided on the farm. I had not had a dinner in two weeks. I headed down to the restaurant that made up the lower portion of the hostel and sat down at the first free table. I had the option between about eight different fish as this small town sat at the confluence of two rivers, both of which flowed east into the Amazon basin, hailing from the snow of the Andes. Villa Tunari was famous for its fresh water fish, especially for country with no ocean. This was a fact I was continually reminded of when I made the mistake of mentioning I came from Chile, who had taken Bolivian ocean access in The War of the Pacific in 1879.

I ordered the typical fish, Pejerrey, and a liter of beer. Strangely enough, as I waited for my food, I noticed the two guys who I'd suspected to be Californians. They invited me to sit with them and I kindly obliged. I soon realized by way of a simple, "Oui" that they hailed from France. Bolivia was absent of any noticeable tourist population except for the French, whose country apparently had many resource-based economic ties to

Bolivia. Later in my trip I realized the Japanese had a great influence on Bolivian roots, but that story can wait. A lively hour of eating fish and drinking wine (on their part) and beer (on mine) ensued. They gave me the gist of the town, said that a fish festival had taken place there the last few days, and notified me that they were running on very little sleep, but made up for any lack of energy with a fish-induced protein supply. They told me to watch out for the chicha, a corn based moonshine equivalent. If I was able to find it, as they had in the fishy revelry of nights past, then one should be particularly careful to sample this drink rather than consume it in copious amounts. It just wasn't good for the stomach, or for the traveler on long trips when there wasn't a wooden toilet available beside the bus driver. I went on to explain to them that I had stopped in this town to catch a day at the monkey refuge, which I'd heard about from some people at the farm. They explained how it was just across the river, how on should get there early to avoid the crowds, and to go with empty pockets because the monkeys were overly-acclimated to humans desire for possessions. Being that they were naturally curious, the monkeys would readily grab your point-and-shoot camera for a bit of reverse tourism.

  I woke up exhausted. The guidebook said to request a room near the back of the hostel to avoid the noisy street in front. I'd chosen to ignore this advice because, at the time, I was too beat to realize whether this was actually the hostel in Bolivia or whether I'd stumbled into a similar joint with the same appellation in Spanish-speaking California. Regardless, I'd been up all night from the barking between two dogs in battle over block supremacy. I packed everything and took some half-finished Spanish language worksheets I'd found at the farm down to breakfast. Breakfast wasn't being served yet. I sat on the hostel balcony peering through a break of subtropical trees realizing that my night's lodging sat on the waterfront. About 15 meters in front of me was the rusted and obsolete aerial cable car that was used to cross the river before the current bridge was built beside it. The rusted lines spanned the 200-meter-wide waterway and were large enough to carry several horses with a wagon or a small truck. This led me to believe that the crossing was constructed when Bolivia first gained access to the emerging world automobile industry. Ironically enough, as of 2008 Evo Morales made a decree that automobiles older than five years would no longer be allowed for import due to air pollution, over-crowdedness and foreign reliance. While this may seem counterintuitive it is actually the older cars that pollute more, retain a greater resale value and that are more readily given as aid once they are deemed 'unusable' due to surpassing a mileage limit for service in their given industrialized nation of origin. I saw some construction workers remodeling the hostel next to mine and wondered how long it might be before they started remodeling the cable car. I wasn't sure if the new bridge would ever collapse, but as I would later see, a common road block would surely make it necessary for an alternate route across the river. In the future this cable car crossing could be a potential local solution to any road block induced political opposition; physically as well as metaphorically speaking.

Then engineering's political-economic advancements, declines, and reuses began to seem trivial. I could feel the cool air rustle past the trees' leaves and thought about how the river carried it down from a much cooler Andean peak, probably less than a day ago.

◎   ◎   ◎

I set out for the monkey, puma, and exotic bird reserve of Inti Wara Yassi. I crossed the bridge and immediately found the front entrance as described to me the night before. The building was amazingly decrepit. I first went to find a place to hang the small advertisement for Ginger's Paradise that I'd designed a few days earlier when the torrential rain prevented me from helping out with any field work at the farm. An old lady, lacking teeth, hair, and height and who appeared to be the matriarchal cook of the small cafeteria, instructed me to hang it on the wall next to some advertisements for animal rights activism. Then I made my way past a herd of about a dozen Gringos (more than I'd seen in my entire time within the borders of Bolivia over the last few weeks). I tried to peel my mind away from the assortment of Americans, Brits, and Aussies, reminding myself that the monkeys were what I came here to see.

I made it to the main ticketing house, and as I checked in my belongings to an empty locker, I began to realize that I was the first visitor of the day. While in the cageless park I would have to rely on my own monkey coping skills. So this was where Anthropology 110 would come in handy? I scolded myself so many times for missing the extracurricular event in that class where an assortment of new world ape skulls was displayed. I'd slept through it, too hung over and just plain tired from drinking the entire night before to bother to attend. *Sigh.* Oh, college. I would make up for it this time, with live specimens nonetheless. If I happened to be in a threatening situation I would just refer to the *Wizard of Oz* flying monkey scene for defense tactics. As I walked past the parrot cages, which were the only cages on the grounds, I heard the sharp, resonating gawk and could only think about the potential danger that faced me on the trail ahead.

I thought back to a story my mother once told me about her childhood. In Girl Scouts, she had gone on a hike in the southern California coastal range. Near Malibu she and her friend broke away from the group and ended up stumbling upon a small village. The small town was comprised of adobe buildings that were situated between oak trees and chaparral brush in the golden hills. The town was absent of people and they discovered it was actually the movie set from *Planet of the Apes.* What would they have done if a guy in a clothed gorilla costume confronted them?

This tangent thought carried me farther away from reality as my lonesome mind wondered congruently with the switchbacks I was currently ascending. What might lie around one corner could very well be either a man in a monkey suit or a reservation monkey. Dr. Zaius could talk. Would these monkeys speak? Would they speak Spanish or English? Obviously Spanish. I'd already figured out animal linguistics by calling several dogs in Spanish and by grilling a parrot for a good five minutes with 'Hello' and

'Hola' at the Santiago Zoo. The parrot eventually answered with 'Hola'. But would these be monkeys or apes that I'd encounter? Certainly there was a difference. I was reminded of the knowledge that was imparted to me in Anthropology 110: monkeys had tails, apes did not. Translation: apes were more like humans. If whatever awaited me had a tail then I should run. But if they're tailless, I should be prepared for a healthy intellectual debate; perhaps even over a nice cup of tea and tobacco pipe like any civilized ape.

I was awakened out of my temporary bout between personification and reality by the squawking of animals in the trees above. What sounded like a high-pitched mix of bird and squirrel noises was actually a half dozen monkeys jumping from limb to limb in the trees above. I had my camera ready and attempted to capture these little guys on film, but they were too quick and too fast, swinging from branch to branch and sometimes even dropping several feet vertically while gaining six or seven feet of forward horizontal progress. Luckily, they were high above me and seemed harmless. In truth, I was overly eager to hold one and had heard they would be eagerly anticipating the arrival of me, Jeff, the giant jungle gym. I decided to get a move on in order to maintain my isolation on the trail. Other visitors would soon enter the park.

I finally ascended to the top of the hill and to a constructed gazebo, a viewpoint that rested in front of a clearing. In front of me was the convergence of two rivers, sitting in a valley that was a patchwork of small farm clearings among an otherwise densely forested background of rolling hills. And in the distance were mountains – the start of the Andean crossing that I would take toward my next destination of Cochabamba. As I looked down on the valley floor at the V-shaped sandbar that lay between the rivers, I noticed a large group enjoying the sunny day. Maybe they were an extended family. They were cleaning their clothes, playing with beach toys, and, although they were far away, I was sure that they had some beach towels from one of the local stores (maybe a Spider-Man towel as I'd seen displayed). These people were completely unaware that they were being watched. My eyes pulled away from the relatively small area the family occupied and began to readjust on the greater valley. With hills in the distance, and jungle immediately surrounding me, I began to think about the level of detail captured in this great frame. There were many things on which I could not focus or realize within this great expanse, nor did I have the metaphysical inclination to think about what might be focusing on the small detail of my being.

Whenever I encounter a difficult situation I try to imagine places like Villa Tunari; how I focused on the small detail of the family on a riverbank and how my vision zoomed out to encompass the whole valley with the endless mountain range on the horizon. I realize how anything affecting my life is literal minutia in relation to the collective happenings of anyone I've ever encountered. I think about how the people on that riverfront evoked such a thought process in myself, though they will never know it. Conversely, I know that something I have done, intentionally or otherwise, has had an effect on someone although I'll never know it.

Photo 8: *A spider monkey watches tourists.*

I set off to finish the trail and find the larger monkeys of the reserve - the spider monkeys. They had no idea I was coming, no idea that the family on the beach had a son with a Spider-Man beach towel, and no reference about the world outside of their reserve boundary. It excited me to know that I was completely outside of the creatures' frame of individual reference, yet a consistent part of their world's daily routine. I'm one other tourist coming here to touch them and gawk at them.

The monos (Spanish for monkeys) ran away from me as I walked down the designated path, others walked toward my general direction in curiosity, and still more approached cautiously right up to my leg. The funniest of all were those that chased one another up tree trunks. Some managed to use their tails to swing through the trees. I noticed the spider monkeys actually had padding on their tails entirely similar to the padding on the inside of their hands so that the appendage amounted to a fifth hand. A couple other monos approached me as I sat on a bench under a branch. They hopped from one limb on the small tree to another and then skipped on over to the top of my back and neck. They'd smelled my cologne and one even licked my neck. The tips of fingers felt like that of a bipedal cat who'd undergone an onychectomy.

Soon the different monkeys found other tourists to be more of a curiosity than me. The park was steadily becoming busier, and almost all of the tourists were wealthy Bolivians who had probably woken at the crack of dawn to make the three-hour drive from Cochabamba, the closet major city capable of giving Mafia-style hair cuts to these gentlemen. I watched as they dangled their used water bottles in front of the monkeys' faces, laughing when the monkeys couldn't open them. They laughed when one of the monkeys took a particular liking to a member of the group. He got a scent from every orifice of the man. All of these monkeys depended on human interaction and, in a sense, these tourists were providing a healthy dose of that from a very different part of Bolivia. But how they teased the poor animals was too much for my taste. I looked at the understaffed monkey rescue volunteers who were already juggling or corralling the other monkey marauders. Outnumbered and outfoxed. The reserve was more like a daycare than anything else. I'd read that the national government was trying to buy out this not-for-profit sanctuary and make it into a public zoo. The monkeys' future in caged exhibits seemed inevitable and the Darwinist in me momentarily faltered; wishing these monkeys could disregard evolution and sprout wings overnight.

◎ ◎ ◎

I was waiting at the bus terminal in Villa Tunari, which was the cheapest option compared to the group taxis one could hire or split between other travelers on any normal American budget. I'd learned this when I asked to hire one; I thought it was only 40 Bolivianos, or 6 bucks, rather than the actual 240 Bolivianos I heard again when my broken understanding of Spanish met his quick salesman speak a second time. I quickly pulled my backpack out of the hired taxi.

The bus station was located between the town's largest beach towel supplier and some locals selling their versions of cart-roasted chicken, wheelbarrow mandarins, and stagnant horchata-type barrel juices. The terminal was surprisingly calm for the day after the large fish festival. I inquired about a smaller and faster shuttle to Cochabamba, as was suggested to me by the Gringos I'd met at the farm. These were relatively more expensive than the cheaper flota bus and took half the time. Tomorrow was Bolivia's 'Dia de Independencia' and I wanted to arrive and get a decent night's rest so I bought the shuttle ticket.

I threw my bags down on the bench and noticed the French guys I'd met were jamming out on an old acoustic while smoking cigarettes. They welcomed me and scooted their bags over so that I could sit by them. They were taking the two o'clock bus – the cheaper option that wouldn't leave for another couple hours. They were just biding their time really without any worry as to when they'd get there. But where was there? Cochabamba too! No kidding. Great, I'm sure I'd see them. I envied their lack of planning and willingness to take the more wallet-friendly option. I told them I'd be off very soon whenever a shuttle was ready to leave.

After an hour of waiting one of them asked me in his broken English, "Why don't you just buy the bus ticket? Only another hour now before it goes..." I transferred my ticket, bought some mandarins and continued to wait.

In the middle of listening to a French nomadic guitar jam I heard the news: all of the roads on the way to Cochabamba were blocked. No one was getting through. Protesters were being paid to block the road on behalf of the eastern separatist government. National presidential recall elections were a week away and they wanted to send a message by stopping the country's logistical infrastructure. I thought back to the farm when I'd talked to Cristobal about political whatever and remembered the disproportionately long conversation we'd had on a subject

I thought only deserved a passing explanation: roadblocks. In his words, "Roadblocks are the way every disagreement is caused and solved in this country."

So I guess I'd be stuck in this dusty town, would eat some more fish, buy a beach towel, and celebrate the Bolivian new year with a couple of French dudes. But the lady selling the tickets was intently speaking with a few of the now sedentary bus drivers. She made an announcement, not to me or my French companions, but directed at the Bolivians at the station. Apparently, smaller cars could get around the roadblocks by driving on berms and non-commercial routes. They'd pack everyone with bus tickets into the smaller shuttles (while charging the bus fare). Within five minutes I was on the road with a maniac driver. He was set on getting back to Villa Tunari that night. This meant he had to go through the roadblocks twice, and I got the impression that they'd be more difficult to traverse as the night went on. Along with Speed Racer, myself, and the French nationals were a Bolivian man and a younger Bolivian couple, who had their dog with them. There was no space to move between the home and garden supplies of the Bolivians and the worldly possessions, including guitar, of my fellow travelers and I.

The three-hour tour took me into a world I hadn't seen previously while traversing the Andes eastward a couple weeks before. That trip had happened under the light of a waning moon, leaving much to the imagination. The weather continually changed as our van made its way up, through and down into various climatic zones. As we passed the small villages the number of 'Evo, Si' banners, dressed in blue and hanging from porch fronts, seemed to increase at a similar frequency to the number of turns in the road, as well as to the speed at which we were wrapping around them.

The jungle basin became the jungle foothills; haystack in appearance and washed green with vegetation. This was puma territory; little to no development given the extreme geography. I stared out the window and saw the untamed wilderness climbing up the haystacks. The mountain mist started to seep over the cracks in the unmaintained road. I had no idea how anyone here could make money.

The residents, then, had two ways in which they could make money. First, they could do what so many other native peoples of Bolivia do to skate by: sell Coca-Cola, packaged chips, and candies to bus travelers at highway checkpoints. It was ironic how those most removed from western-style consumerism in their own lives were forced to sustain themselves by selling these corporate goods to the consumption dependent tourists. The other option was trafficking. Sure, you could do cocaine trafficking, but I hadn't seen this with my own eyes. Instead, I watched as a man flagged us down on the side of the road. I'm still unsure how the driver noticed him, it didn't seem like he'd taken notice to anything outside his tunnel vision until then. We came to a complete stop and the driver opened the passenger side window. The man had a package and it seemed like he just needed a ride to deliver it. Fair enough, but we didn't have any seats. Wrong. A few seconds later we were off and he had squeezed between the conductor and young man up front to straddle the gear stick. We dropped him off after about 20 minutes of driving but the driver kept his money and his package. Immediately after the man exited the driver instructed the young man next to him to open the package. It was a Coca-Cola bottle filled with some liquid. The willing passenger took a small taste. He nodded to the driver. Was it chicha, the corn-based moonshine type thing common around here, or something else? To this day I don't know, but it was probably never delivered. At the next checkpoint the inspections officer asked if we were carrying anything illegal. The shuttle driver quickly handed over the package, but no money.

We descended from the summit of the highway down the western side of the cordillera, going around hairpin turns and passing semis in near solid mist. The mist turned into patchy blue skies and then again into near-solid sun. We passed by a hay truck that was tipped over just after a tight turn. No doubt the truck had driven too fast but I wasn't sure of the reasons behind its urgency. Perhaps it was trying to beat the construction of roadblocks which were showing up with more and more frequency throughout the country as the midterm recall election grew closer. The men who funded the roadblock construction that was used to suspend food and necessary supplies from reaching select cities were the same men who wanted to control their own natural gas profits instead of sharing the wealth between all Bolivia's citizens for basic health and education needs. These were also the same men who wanted Evo and his social reform out of office.

6. Cochabamba

The giant statue of Cristo de la Concordia appeared in the distance. This most famous landmark of Cochabamba stands 33 meters tall on the highest hill of the third largest city in Bolivia. Mere minutes passed as our mini van drew closer to the city. As we drove closer the statue didn't change much, which alluded to its massive size. After three hours in a cramped (albeit new) van, my butt was sore and my legs were begging for mobility. I kept readjusting, switching my weight from one cheek to the other. The golden hills we descended from reminded me of my native California, only lacking the oak trees that spotted the water-rich creases of the hills. The rolling hills gave way to exurban farming plots, small allotments clearly not on a scale to reap profits, but tenable for family essentials like maize and potatoes. These, in turn, grew closer together until it was apparent we'd reached what were the suburbs of the Cochabamba municipality that held over 600,000 people.

Our small van reached a giant intersection, all four sides courted off. Concrete roadblocks, rocks of various sizes, vehicles, and scrap metal were among the random items that the paid protesters had strewn across the multi-lane artery. The van took an abrupt right and navigated its way by alleyway, zigzagging through the grid development in an effort to avoid the other buses, trucks, and cars who were attempting the same counter plan. More than once, we encountered an unworkable route and had to backtrack. After nearly half an hour, and a worsening sense of nausea, we finally arrived at a roundabout that was fully circulating traffic. Like clockwork. Our driver's intensity reached a critical mass as he pushed us into the constant flow of one side and shot us out on the opposing end. Soon we arrived in the middle of a busy market and the van stopped. This was certainly not a bus terminal, nor a parking space, but rather in the middle of the road. We jumped out and grabbed all our belongings. I was ready to find a hostel and I set out on foot for my lodging that night. The next morning I decide to check out the La Concha open-air market. It was reputed to be the largest of its kind in all the country! Coca leaf vendors were scattered between wholesale grain, meat and textile brokers. I bought a bag from a woman who appeared to be completely blind and as old as the coca trade herself. She made me measure out the leaves for her and felt my paper money. Her blindness begot an aura of trust and magic as she returned the correct change. I bought a little bicarbonate tar to chew with my leaves. It serves as a catalyst to bring out the full coca alkaloid-heightening effects that counters altitude sickness.

Immediately I started to chew, as I sought relief from the altitude-induced fatigue and headache from which I was currently suffering. There were a dozen or so fruits I'd never seen in my life. Some strewn on blankets over the concrete, others in the laps of women, and still more stacked on large tables. A bulbous indigenous woman pushing a wheelbarrow-load of bread also carried a baby on her back. She pushed in between myself and a truck which was honking its horn at the crowd on the other side of her. The woman pushed a cart full of bread rolls. I needed some food and sat down to a vendor who was selling a grain soup called sopa de trigo. I wanted was a little soup at 10:30 in the morning but instead I got enough to fill me for the day. It came with salad, rice, a potato, and a side of beef 'al pobre'; literally meaning poor but actually consisting of an egg on top. This was definitely a result of my poor Spanish. At least it only cost me a buck for everything.

It was Bolivian Independence Day and I decided to go out that night to get a head start on the holiday, but to my surprise everyone else in the city had the same idea. In Bolivia, they celebrate the holiday the night before, which makes sense when you want to party on the night before you have the whole day off to recuperate. I walked towards the central plaza where I assumed the activities would take place and witnessed an endless parade full of soldiers, high school bands, and drill teams with uncharacteristically tall Bolivian girls. Everyone was out in force. Little boys on their fathers' shoulders. Young couples eating cotton candy. Groups of teenage boys sitting on the park bench checking out girls.

Photo 9: Foosball tables set up on the street for players during Dia de Independencia festivities.

The turnout surprised me. While La Paz and Sucre were both larger they were also both the joint capitals, one being the administrative seat and the latter being the constitutional and judicial seat. This city didn't have any claim to national decision-making status. This national pride was pure, unadulterated love for a country that was currently on the cusp of civil unrest. But I was safe in the unified zone that sought one Bolivia for all. This was the highlands; this was Evo Morales country.

I continued, pushing through the crowd and made it to the main plaza where a variety of pastries, fried food, and candy were being sold. Yup. Just like the U.S. There were even some hippies selling their beads and jewelry. It was the dreaded French guy! We chatted it up for a bit, but reached the limit of each other's second language after only a couple minutes. I wished him well and kept walking, following the parade route. The air was filled with continual music from the marching bands. As I moved forward, one band's chorus became another's verse. Trumpets changing to drums.

I saw six or seven foosball tables set up in a row. Somehow these tables were much more legitimate in a country that considered soccer to be a source of national pride. I had memories of playing foosball in my middle school game room. We called it the Falcon's Nest, after our mascot. Since then no matter if I'd played at someone's house or in a bar, the same rule always came up: no spins! You couldn't cup your hands around the handle and spin the soccer figures continually in an effort to hit the ball so fast that the opponent wouldn't be able to defend. Spins are a true handicap move, often invoked in desperation or due to lack of skill. These kids I noticed didn't use the spinning technique. Their soccer skill had transferred over from foot to finger. I stood at the end of the tables that were lined up in a row. It looked like one long soccer game, fingers maneuvering, elbows flailing and heads turning left to right in an unordered pattern, following each of their balls, different for each game. Just watching this made me fatigued and hungry.

I hadn't eaten a solid meal in over a day. I was craving a burrito so I went to a 'Mexican' chain restaurant, mentioned in Lonely Planet, and got a huge, dry, and chicken-filled burrito. It was like they wrapped up a whole chicken in a burrito. I was already feeling sold out over the very American dining experience; posters for different American movies, pictures of sports stars, and promotional black and whites of celebrities blanketed the wall. I was on the second story of a sit-down fast food joint that served everything from pizza to burritos to espresso to frozen yogurt.

When a 'theme' restaurant tries for too many differing themes by covering the walls in just about anything then it suffers from what I like to call the 'Applebees Effect'. Many of today's themed restaurants like to cover their walls in newly weathered items. Go into an Applebees anywhere and you'll see the fabricated history for whatever city is listed on the highway exit sign. They'll have the old high school football jersey hanging next to a picture of some unnamed folks, too old to recognize, who used to run the town. On the other wall will be some trophies from years past, and other artifacts like an old barber shop or cobbler sign that make the place seem historic, and by default, original. But then go to an Applebees in another state and you'll see the same cookie-cutter design and artifacts covering the wall, save for the different jersey of that town's local high school football team. Here I was in the Applebees of Bolivia eating factory-farmed chicken, watching the obese of the nation file in for a quasi-celebratory dinner. Worst of all, this wasn't even a Mexican burrito. A lot people who haven't been to South America don't realize it, but the burrito is wholly Mexico's creation and can't be readily found south of Panama. Being from California I believe I have a pretty good idea of what qualifies as a burrito. This was no burrito. This was an imitation of an imitation: an American themed establishment advertising itself as a purveyor of Mexican burritos, all the while located in Bolivia. I'm all about fusion cuisine but there was no fusion, just cheap duplication and certainly no cuisine.

The dry burrito gave me a thirst and so I wandered until I found a quaint bar that was playing Pink Floyd videos on T.V. screens, had walls adorned with artsy murals, and where a live jazz band was playing. I got down a trago, a mixed drink of the local flavor that had alcohol distilled from grapes, and sat. I was tired and sick. I should have gone home at that point. Instead I found another bar. I noticed some girls that looked Gringa and bought a Cuba libre, rum and coke, just so I could ask them, "Good sangria?" I felt invisible as I sat by myself drinking down Castro's tears. I asked where they were from because they sounded Eastern European. They never responded but, in truth, I don't think they heard over the music. Regardless, Cuba had never seemed so far away from freedom to me. I headed back to the hostel after I had my mind set on going to bed, but hit up the original bar for one last drink. I had two issues; I was indecisive and alone. All this arose because I wanted to meet people, but either way I'd sacrificed my health. I wandered back to my closet or so called single occupancy room with its creaky bed and went to sleep with my legs dangling over the edge. Tired. Ill. Alone.

    The next day I woke up and headed for the market in hopes of discovering a more authentic meal than I'd found the night before. The meal I found wasn't breakfast or lunch. It was 10:30 in the morning and I was the only customer present aside from a young family in the other corner of the small food stall who, judging by there quick order, must have been regulars. What I ate didn't look like a breakfast or lunch. In my head I gave the meal a title of des-almuerzo, which I took from combining the Spanish words for breakfast and lunch in an attempt to make a word in Spanish for brunch. I paid then wandered around the market past supposed witches. The stalls held, among other medicinals, many different llama fetuses which varied in size and hair content; near embryonic to fetal, bald to hairy locks. Then I wandered through the meat section where I found baby chickens hanging on a line, skinned, and without feathers waiting to go onto someone's grill. I never figured that anyone would eat baby chick meat; there just wasn't enough.

The market changed shape, through different booths, streets, and city blocks. I walked around for nearly an hour with no end in sight. I walked by a man selling TVs, then an entire city block of plastic Chinese toy sellers, followed a consortium of textile sellers, checker boarded together under a giant canopy. Soon I was back to the food section where I started. I pulled out my guidebook to get bearings. I'd go to the archaeological museum and take a tour. It was about a 30-minute walk and I would arrive just in time for the first tour of the day.

I arrived at the museum to find it closed. It was, after all, a holiday, so I sat down and chewed on some coca leaves that I was keeping handy in my day pack. I folded them in my mouth with my tongue to get a solid wad to mix with the bicarbonate. As I was staring down into my bag of leaves Thomas, the French guy with the better English and shorter hair, walked up. His appearance surprised me since he told me the other day that he was going to get out of Cochabamba quickly. I extended my bag of coca leaves and he graciously accepted. I was happy to be picking up South American greeting customs but figured a friendly sharing gesture was pretty universal. We sat there and chewed as I thumbed through my guidebook. He explained to me that no buses were running due to the holiday. Stuck and sick he'd caught me on his way to find a doctor's office. I suggested a tearoom to sooth our sore throats and soon we were off.

I held the guidebook like a compass. We found a upscale joint that shooed away the panhandlers who accosted us throughout our tea time. First it was a nine-year-old boy wanting to shine Thomas' shoes, then a middle-aged women with a baby wrapped in the blanket around her back, followed by an old man that shuffled from table to table on a gimp leg. Each person was promptly told to leave the restaurant balcony by the staff. The whole street seemed to be upscale. I noticed the table next to me was full of a group of young Gringos who were holding hands in prayer. They ate their assorted sushi, pasta, and burger dishes. I never saw them give any money to the beggars. In simple English words I told Thomas how I didn't like places that gentrified and excluded what was otherwise public domain. He calmly stated that we would all have to go back to our own countries sometime and went on to say that he makes an effort to seek out places like this that are a little more upscale just to remind himself of home. I wasn't sure if he was speaking as a true French food connoisseur or a man who found solace in familiar food. However, he was right; it was a reminder of one's roots. Grounding yourself periodically can be healthy when in another culture because it gives you time to reflect on how different that culture is from your own.

We finished our tea and headed back to our respective hostels. A couple Bolivian teenage girls asked for our picture with some boys who they were babysitting. It was refreshing to realize I stuck out that much. I was starting to forget. The situation reminded me of the time I was visiting my college buddy in Japan. We were at a pagoda garden when a harem of young Japanese schoolgirls confronted us and asked for a picture with the two of us. My friend Brent conjectured, "But we're not celebrities," to them in Japanese. Of course this didn't matter, so we posed as their school leader took a picture of us with each of their 12 cameras.

I returned to the hostel to grab some money and a quick nap. The cat nap lasted 20 minutes at best, and I left the hostel through the same door through which I entered. What had been a quiet street 20 minutes prior was now full of an entire company of the Bolivian Army's ski troopers. There were seven or eight buses along with a couple hundred men in white snow suits and giant supply packs that were mingling throughout the street. Such a strange sight in the otherwise sunny and quiet day. Later on I caught another, what seemed to be, impromptu parade and saw these soldiers marching with their muskets.

I took off to catch a double feature of *The Dark Knight* and *Hancock* at the theater. Earlier that day the man at the cinema insisted one movie was in English and the other would have subtitles. I met Thomas at the movie theater and we enjoyed a double feature matinée with both movies dubbed in standard Castellano Spanish. I was fine with both movies being in Castellano but utterly disappointed with my lack of prescience when it came to seeing a blow off in another language. I'd heard the ticketing agent correctly but he must've thought it easier to answer yes to my question.

I spent one more day in Cochabamba hoping to see some sites but again everything was closed. It seemed that in this country a holiday meant the days preceding and succeeding too. I woke up and grabbed a yogurt shake with some granola. If there's one thing I could take from that corner of the world, that city and that block it would giant yogurt shakes, mixed with whichever fruits you desired and served with granola. I've yet to find an equal! I suppose I could try to duplicate such a delicacy here in the U.S., but I can tell you that I wouldn't be able to make it for a dollar, which is roughly what I paid there. walked around in the same clothes I'd been wearing for the last couple of days. My laundry was currently in a laundromat, getting pressed and dry-cleaned. This was the only option that I could find for a laundromat, and was relatively inexpensive. Absolutely necessary as my clothes were covered in mud, trees, coffee beans, and cow milk from the last couple weeks of farming.

I decided to try some market food for lunch, at a smaller market only a block away from the hostel. I had the hardest time finding a place that would serve me a soup at three in the afternoon. I asked around at every stall but they all told me it was past soup time. Finally one lady waved her hands at me. I could tell she sensed my confusion and wanted my business but had gone out of her way to cater to me. I received a soup, a main course, and a salad. I was beat. It seemed like the best meal ever but they all do when you're traveling and fatigued. After my meal was done I tipped her one extra Boliviano but she seemed confused. No one tipped at these types of places and she probably thought I didn't understand the price. I was excited to head to Bolivia's capital of La Paz in the morning. From what I'd heard, it was full of Gringos, an unfamiliar sight since I'd left Chile. The Gringos I could deal with; I was one of them. What surprised me, however, were the ninjas.

Photo 10: Ski patrol soldiers suiting up for the Dia de Independencia parade.

I always thought Bruce Lee would have the upper hand on Chuck Norris. Whether it was an ingrained sense of heroism for the iconic martial artist, or the result of growing up as an American boy who liked to play ninjas in the school yard, or even my waning opinion of Mr. Norris since he'd given his support for GOP Presidential candidate Mike Huckabee; I couldn't say. But I found myself watching a twenty-something, fully shaved, Chuck Norris waling on Bruce Lee amongst some Roman ruins.

My day had already been tough enough. For starters, the woman next to me smelled like she hadn't showered in weeks. If she'd stayed on her corner of the seat I could've avoided her stench, but she took up her own seat along with half of mine. What she lacked in height was certainly made up for in a horizontal measurement nearly equal to her foot to forehead distance. This resulted in a general rotundity that wasn't suited for your traditional bus seat. As I looked around I noticed that this was the case with many of the other women who occupied the bus. They shared a few similar features: all wore brightly colored dresses with lace trim along the fabric endings, they had two braided pigtails, and on top of each woman's head sat a black bowler hat. I was a bit hesitant to part with my belongings but thought it was courteous to stow my backpack below the bus. In my lap I carried a travel book, extra-starchy bread rolls and bottled water. The maiden to my left chose to bring her standard family-size bottle of Coca-Cola, three hand-loomed blankets that were filled so as to be used as sacks and two full cardboard boxes. All of these were carefully balanced between her legs and on her lap, overlapping my leg room and the greater part of my seat. I stand as a six-foot, three-inch man and found it difficult to balance on one cheek, in the small, crowded seats for six hours. I stared out the window, secretly redirecting my eyes so I could figure out where she ended and where her clutter began. Surely they were one. I wasn't sure why she hadn't utilized the cargo space below and was a bit annoyed with the predicament I found myself in. But I was left admiring the woman for her monk-like ability to keep still and circus-like ability to balance.

I shifted my body to the right and looked out the window, on the other side of the aisle, away from my neighbor's Jenga-like mass. I was caught in the midst of a grandfather to grandson bonding session before my eyes could make it to the window. The grandson vomited into a tin can, with oil colored drool tethering his mouth to the tin while his grandfather balanced him on one knee and chewed coca leaves. Each bite of his jaw pushed up the ledge of his cheek bone once more and with it the old man's spongy face exuded an aurora of steadfastness unparalleled to anything I'd ever seen. He was a veteran and was patiently teaching a lesson to his uninitiated heir. The boy was around 60 pounds and the grandfather couldn't have been more than twice his weight. There would be room for the boy to grow. Both in mass and skill. The road was becoming curvier.

The woman's meditative balancing act and the old man's oscillating jaw both seemed to work well against any road induced sickness. I knew by the cold draft against my unseated right rear cheek that the bus was ascending to higher elevations and that more layers over my body would be required. My eyes made it past the multitude of distractions within the bus to the world outside. I saw the first snow adapted creature of my journey; it was a black, white and brown cow. It stood alone in the middle of a snow drift and dirt field. I saw no other reason for this cow to be here except to fertilize the future crop of dirt with his nitrogen-rich mystic dung. He too was adapted. A veteran of many winters, in a meditative state chewing whatever grain he was given with the same mechanized jaw of the old man. My visual stimuli refocused on the most similar color combination within my peripheral vision: Chuck Norris in white, Bruce Lee in black, amongst a stone brown background of Roman ruins. Like the snow on the cow's back, Bruce had the upper hand. I watched for the ensuing minutes as the final fight scene of the movie came to an end. Chuck was knocked out in one fell swoop. He was the novice. I looked around to see who else was as excited as me and I nearly jumped into the lap that existed somewhere in the heap of blankets and woman to my left. But no one was taken by the movie playing on the small video screen at the front of the bus. The final fight scene of two modern-day ninjas was the only thing distracting me from bitter cold and nausea; a movie-cum-coping method. I was no veteran, just a well traveled couch potato. Certainly I was a guest in a bus, and in a country, full of much more resilient people. Without choice they balanced and chewed. They had something that I didn't: experience.

7. The Peace

We neared El Alto and I began to see farmland become dotted with churches, noted by their colonial-style steeples. Cows were replaced by small rundown buildings trying to pass for residences. The houses catered to necessity rather than desire and were shy of the amenities many Americans would hold dear: the lawn gnome, a paved driveway, green lawn, attached garage and maybe a welcome mat with a saying like 'Come Back with a Warrant'. Now I was in a suburban hodgepodge of buildings with streets jutting off from the larger arterial we'd taken. El Alto was a city in its own right but referred to as a suburb when spoken in reference to La Paz. Bolivia's administrative capital city, La Paz, had exploded since its humble beginnings as a Spanish mining outpost, sending development up its valley walls and overflowing into the surrounding plateau. El Alto, however, lacked the key characteristics that mark a North

American suburb. There were no cul-de-sacs. There were no street or development signs named after the trees, animals, or native culture that they'd replaced; like 'Redwood Estates' or 'Deer Lake Golf Course'. There were certainly no gated communities. There were, however, cookie-cutter houses! The McMansion of Bolivia was more aptly the McShack/McMarket jointly made for living and selling your wares, repeated many times over, and constructed as a low-cost box structure. Many buildings remained unfinished with rebar sticking out of their studs like a misaligned protruding bone after some terrible accident.

The bus came to an abrupt stop in the middle of a crowded market. The women in traditional dresses, twice as wide as the aisles they stood in, stumbled forward under the weight of their heavy sacks. One woman's hat slipped off her head, exposing the meticulously parted origins of her braids. The majority of the passengers left at the stop preceding La Paz proper, revealing their meager roots. As I stared out the window in some kind of stupor, my eyes began to focus on a line that stretched to its block-long terminus, originating from what looked like a social crediting agency. More directly in front of my window were old women sitting with blankets strewn out on the dirt street. The throws were dotted with small supplies of fruit or hygienic supplies. It was a testament to the economics of necessity. I thought back to my college economic classes. This was a microcosm of the greater economy. This was how economies took shape.

The bus began heading down into the more affluent lowlands, sitting just shy of 12,000 ft. I could feel the pull and tug of the gears as the bus eased to a complete stop in order to pay the highway entrance fee required by the municipality. This would be the last time I'd feel any such braking mechanism during my three-day stay in La Paz, which was a city marked by weaving roads, blind corners and heavy foot traffic. Upon descending into Bolivia's most densely populated city, I immediately saw that there were skyscrapers coalesced in the lowest part of the bowl. As arguably South America's least developed country, this was a sight I hadn't seen or necessarily expected in the preceding month of intra-national travel. The height of the skyscrapers slowly waned into the typical multi-story and multi-use buildings of any urban configuration, and then again into single-story residences. The lessening architectural height and the countervailing rise in the geologic altitude of the valley walls seemed to turn what would otherwise be a bowl into a shapelier frying pan or wok, where all the contents were piled in the center to simmer under the close sun. The bus weaved through a patch of trees as we continued descending and I was reminded of the once lush valley. I'm sure that if every person occupying this dense city was instead a tree, less me, then I would have been able to walk across the valley, tree top to tree top, without ever setting foot on the ground. I imagined how I might do this in rapid descent, then cross over, hopping between pines and gum trees, then up again onto the opposing ridge, all the while being fueled in the otherwise thin air by the oxygen rich output of such forgotten wooden relics.

My coach reached the terminal in the late afternoon and I immediately exited, fearing that my backpack would be, or had already been, pawned to an advantageously-positioned local. To my elation, all 60 lbs of my pack were there. I slung it over my shoulder and have never felt as much like an urban sherpa as I did at the time. In the three o'clock sun I was bundled in multiple layers to avoid the chill that was rampant in any locale which sat nearly two miles ASL. My pack hung to one side, adjusted for the uneven weight distribution on my wary shoulders. I perused the lobby of a hostel not far from the bus depot. It had caught my attention for having, according to my guidebook, the highest microbrewery in the world. Actually, they were just a few blocks down the hill from Bolivia's largest macro brewery and appropriately marketed their unique, relatively low-production, micro brew status in order to gain their highest brewery in the world title. The place seemed nice, however I'm not one to make a decision without first seeing the comparison. I hopped in a taxi and headed for the next hostel on my list. This was recognized as the highest Irish pub in the world. Looking back on it, the guidebook I used showed most of the hostels there with a self-proclaimed feat to best any other hostel. I was a little surprised I hadn't found the hostel with the highest bunk bed, or highest staircase, but then realized these were probably disadvantageous for the intrepid but highly un-acclimated, twenty-something boozer/traveler who made up the majority of the international clientèle. My taxi driver let me off about a block away from my hostel and told me this was the location. I paid him and walked down the street to the correct lodging. The hostel had all the amenities, including beer and a pool table. I was beat and I decided to take a bottom bunk in an eight person double gender dorm. After I locked up my pack I went straight up to the bar to order a drink and write in my journal. Predictably, but not necessarily what my travel-trodden body would've liked, one beer turned into many more. The Irish bar had full service: plenty of grub, a stocked bar, and a convenient tab direct to your hostel bill. The last feature would be a downfall for myself and many other patrons. Halfway through the night when I suddenly realized that I was surrounded entirely by English speakers when I reached the level of inebriation that begets an alcohol-induced epiphany. I'd heard some Dutch and a bit of German, both first languages to those speaking them, but never a complete sentence of Spanish. Irish was the prevailing dialect here, followed by some British slang and humor. As a matter of fact, I hadn't met one other American in any of the random introductions forced upon me by chance, proximity, or sheer awkwardness. Here I was completely immersed in the cultural and working capital of the most indigenously rich nation of the South American continent, and it was college-aged study abroad/Euro-vacation all over again.

My excitement, however, continued to build with every conversation about the local activity, be it market or archaeological exploration, that I would soon be undertaking once the predicted hangover subsided. After talking with several people in the bar, it seemed like there were three or four favorite activities. Only later, after I continued on the same path, did I realize that the reason everyone had done the same things was that they, too, would hang in the bar at night and wake up late in the day to take a trip organized by the hostel's own travel agency. The perfect, unassuming, business model. Most of these people would never have to step beyond the comforts and accessibility that the hostel offered. The ease of access was astonishing but catered to an ever-growing disparity between local experience and tourism. For the first time on my trip I felt like a tourist. I had arrived at the start of the Gringo Trail. I didn't leave the hostel until the next morning. Actually, early afternoon.

This day is blank from my memory. A testament to the high altitude and shenanigans of the night before. I woke with a sore throat that was probably caused by the smoggy air that seemed to layer the altitudinous valley like loose saran wrap that had sunk into a bowl after another dish had been set upon it. I passed the day by catching up on my emails to family and possible graduate schools. That evening I rewound my life's track and hit play at the same spot: in the bar. Absolute repeat, except now I had some solid plans, and accordingly was set to wake up on schedule to follow them. I set my phone alarm for noon. The phone I carried didn't receive service outside of Chile but provided me with an alarm, a couple pixel games, and most importantly a flashlight. I used my flashlight phone to thumb through my belongings as quietly as possible in a room where others had already laid down for the night, and crawled into bed as the sun began to rise.

On my travel schedule I couldn't bring myself to sleep in past nine, and had been up shuffling around the hostel's creaky wooden floors for a few hours waiting to go to prison. I'd heard of San Pedro Prison, but was skeptical about the actual feasibility of entering a secured prison, or more aptly leaving that prison. One could pay a guard to get in to the fortress that stood in the center of the busy capital but as a foreigner how could I really be assured of an exit? I needed an exit strategy and, as an American living in era of failed Middle East invasions, I realized this was not my strength. Nevertheless, I'd met a few people who'd paid the guards to enter the section of the prison where they kept foreign drug crime and other felony-level offenders. I'd heard that the inmates were amiable and truly wanted to educate travelers about daily prison life. Most of the offenders were there for drug-related trafficking crimes and as such I'd heard that the incarcerated offered whiskey and more illicit substances at an inflated price.

 We exited the hostel and stepped onto the stone paved road, emerging into the sunny but cool air. I walked over to the prison with my two British friends, whom I'd met the night before, and stopped to buy some nuts and bottled water. If there was one thing I wouldn't buy in the prison, it was food. I found an ATM and withdrew 250 Bolivianos. This was the equivalent of about $45 American and the amount of money I would need to pay off the guards or purchase any illegalities inside the prison, be it for my own desire or for the appeasement of any deranged inmate. Hey, a guy in jail needs to make a living somehow, right?

We wandered up some side streets; slowly gaining elevation as the streets meandered past seemingly-regular buildings. Wouldn't a prison look different? "There it is!" I barked. "No, that's a school," said the Brit. He'd already been there twice in the preceding days. A cockney guy through and through, he mumbled in his guttural voice about his fascination with a couple of the inmates. He went on about their snorting problems, their mental illnesses, and how they were plainly screwed over since all of them he'd talked to were foreigners. He made it clear, though, that since they didn't have any rights they were free to do whatever they wanted. They had their own key to their cell and would pay off the guards to smuggle, drugs, booze, and tourists inside. They were completely free, except to leave.

In front of us where the weaving path split was a building, pink with stucco and decrepit from years of neglect. The walls were bare and high. I couldn't see inside but figured the sheer height may be the only mechanism discouraging any prison breaks. A dark green door appeared at the end of the tan stucco wall. A guard emerged with a gun thrown around his vest. The cockney guy, wearing a classic soccer windbreaker, asked cordially about how we might go about entering by hinting at our money. The guard turned him down and told us that today everything was closed. Due to the upcoming elections, there was a heightened sense of security. No one was getting in or out. In a prison? Who would've thought? Honestly, I was disappointed. We walked around and tried to find another way in, looking into the main gate, where the actual Bolivian prisoners were being let out. There I gained an appreciation for what it might be like. I looked around while standing by the main entrance and saw the despots of La Paz, waiting for their family members or drunken friends to emerge from a night of jail, only to make their financial situation worse. People were moaning and yelling. The guards had guns in hand, the walls of the prison were falling apart, and inmates remained in their tattered street clothes. I wondered what lie behind those crumbling walls. What was the real hell that my eyes would never see? But I was free, and so were my friends. We walked off and decided to take in a view of the whole city. On our free day we would grab some ice cream and embrace the nomadic and vagrant lifestyle. Plans can change just like that, especially when you have the time and money to make them happen, not to mention the freedom.

We headed up to the Mirador, or view point, by alleyway and staircase where I was sure no vehicle could fit. It was a strenuous ascent that required taking off some clothing layers and one that made me hungry. Little ice cream bins were on every street's corner store. Passing the kiosks, one after the other, we slowly discovered that the "Rocky" brand bars were less expensive the higher we climbed. It surprised me that food should be cheaper in the hills, but I soon realized that no one would make this hike and exert so much energy just to save $0.50. La Paz is unlike most cities in America. The hills house the less affluent peoples, while the valley is where the wealthy live. Due to the high altitude, any uphill walking requires substantial effort, even for those accustomed to the task. So the poor are relegated to valley walls where it is harder to build, harder to breathe, and harder to live. Though I believe the destitute end up winning in this situation thanks to their view.

We arrived at the lookout point and there was nothing more beautiful than seeing that sporadic development. It was as if the city was crawling up towards the sun, and blooming where it found air. I took in the view with my camera and my eyes, recording what I saw now and saving it for later, panorama style. The geographer in me truly enjoys viewing cities from above: in Paris at the Eiffel Tower, in Tokyo on the 34th story of an office building, and in Seattle at the Space Needle. All these landmarks offered a unique bird's eye view of the planning, or lack thereof, that went into a city. Seeing the form of parallels and discontinuity that compliment each other in opposing ways helps render the cityscape into a living and breathing character that is always in the process of change. Although so many cities can be seen in a negative light as being environmentally degrading due to their excess in consumption and waste, I have come to appreciate cities as microcosms of their region and people's combined culture. Looking down at La Paz I could see the soccer stadium to my left, the winding river flowing down the middle, the newer city center with its skyscrapers below, and on the opposing hills, houses that gazed back at me. La Paz should have never been a capital city due to its geographic isolation, high altitude, and poor climate but was built up to primacy in the years following the initial Spanish silver mining. I was staring at a piecemeal pattern of development. Each lot's growth fed off another's demise, each market's profit was another's loss, and the erection of each church steeple denoted the religious loss of a few more native inhabitants.

The next day, Wednesday, I again woke up hung over. There were two more days for me in La Paz and I decided that I needed to be as productive as possible. Whatever this meant, I knew one thing: no sitting in the hostel. So I left on my own and decided to explore the city some more. Eventually I found a more affluent area on the east end. There was even an ice cream parlor there. I stepped inside but in my excitement and confusion, a yuppie family with their little kid managed to cut in front of me without asking so much as if I was waiting to order. Okay, so I still looked like a tourist. Great to know. I bought my ice cream and continued along past some urban murals that were probably commissioned by the city because they fit neatly within their concrete frames. I found a dog sitting in a patch of sun on the middle of the sidewalk. He was soaking it up without any regard for the busy foot traffic which hopped over him.

Walking down La Paz's main street, El Prado, I encountered some drinking pals from the hostel bar who I'd met on one of the past few nights. We lay on the grass for a while until someone suggested we try to either find some election riots or get a better look at the city. There was still nothing open due to the midterm reelection or, more aptly, recall that was initiated by the right-leaning autonomous Governor of Department (Province) Santa Cruz. Although Santa Cruz wasn't wholly autonomous, the rest of the country had little say in what went on in the region, save for the government ownership of land and resources that was proposed in the resource-rich East. Under Evo Morales, the country's first indigenous President, Bolivia was heavily divided into generalizations: indigenous or European-descending populations; western highland Andeans or eastern lowland Amazonian; socialists or capitalists; and producers or consumers. The division and current election meant two things for me: no beer and nothing open. Fortunately the hostel bar where I was staying continued to serve and since everything was closed it meant I had to do my own exploring, which I was always game for.

Photo 11: Ferris wheel cable weaving.

After two hours of walking around aimlessly the group of us found the one thing open: a kids' fair complete with mini Ferris wheel. To that day I'd never ridden a Ferris wheel. It was time to change things. A girl at the hostel, Skye, and I hopped into a mini cage and had the door locked behind us. I explained to her that this would be my first time on a Ferris wheel. Aussie through and through, she insisted, "That's okay mate." The ride stopped and started every ten seconds as someone else got on or wanted off. Finally after about five minutes we had a continuous rotation. We laughed and I began to feel comfortable. Then as we passed where the operator stood, we could see him working intently on something. Another go-round and we saw him threading together the cable that drove the spinning wheel. All of the times my parents had warned me about cheap carny rides had been for not. I'd always been overly-cautious when it had come to carnival rides that were strung together in a couple days' time and then taken apart for the next show. I'd foolishly let my guard down in La Paz Little did I think I would die on a Ferris wheel, and now this ride was coming undone. I would have liked to trust the operator and believe that his hands were professional weaving machines, but didn't know how often this mishap occurred. I wouldn't just sit there and be thrown off a Ferris wheel. I still had another month of traveling! With each rotation Skye and I used our weak Spanish skills to convey a desire to stop and exit. We went through several different forms of exit, stop and finish in Spanish until after four more rotations he considered it convincing enough to stop the ride. We exited the cage, Skye paid the attendant, and it was back to the hostel for a late afternoon nap.

When I awoke the sun had set on Bolivia, but had it also set on a revolutionary leader's political era? I wondered about the elections results while I emerged from the cave that was my dorm and into the bustle of the normal hostel traffic. I was fatigued not so much from the long days but from the asynchronous sleep patterns. Immediately I was confronted by a man with a 35-mm camera around his neck and a girl, both of whom I'd shared a couple drinks with in the nights leading up to this one. "Have you heard? Evo won the vote! We're going to watch him give an acceptance speech right now at the Presidential Palace," he said in his Gaelic accent. The British girl added, "Wanna come?" Believe me, I thought about it long and hard in the matter of a few hundred milliseconds. My mouth was moving, when my brain caught up with an emphatic, "Si!" We ran out the door and headed up four short blocks to the main governmental center of Plaza Murillo.

The soldier presence increased as we neared the brightly-lit plaza. We shuffled past the gaze of some attentive police to get a better look. Ahead was the back of the main stage, projecting onto the plaza. We were behind the action and took some pictures from this unique perspective of the crowd, which consisted of almost entirely indigenous peoples. Then in an effort for a better camera angle the camera guy I was with chanced his luck and jumped another barricade. This time a soldier with an AK-47 stepped in front of the Irish photographer. We'd have to walk around an entire square block to gain access to the plaza.

Fifteen minutes later we were positioned in the middle of the crowd. I did my best to avoid blocking anyone's view but my efforts were fruitless; I stood a whole half meter above most everyone else. My height offered me a unique vantage point. The people packed the plaza and waved banners, signs, indigenous flags, the presidential flag, and national flags. The occasional vendors parted the revelers with their waving arms full of even more rally gear.

It was a sea of direct democracy. Because of these people, Evo had managed to narrowly surpass the percentage of the vote needed to re-validate his presidency; about 54 percent. He'd won the first election at this percentage and it was obvious that the reelection process was authored by his political adversaries who knew that it'd be difficult to receive this again rather than a simple plurality. The opposition had counted on the record numbers of indigenous peoples who voted for Evo originally to remain complacent on this day. In the weeks leading up to the election the Right used road blocks to deter commerce from entering and exiting the larger cities. They had hoped to disrupt commerce and change minds, but the hope to curtail voter turnout had failed.

I felt fire in the sky and saw a small hot air balloon, fueled by a rudimentary fire propulsion system, floating above the crowd and trailing off into the cold night. The blue and white stripes on the balloon, reflecting Evo's Presidential flag, gave way to a slogan I saw everywhere that night: *Evo, Si!* A person in a giant condor costume was dancing along with two blue bull-costumed dancers. They fluttered and charged around the main stage, dancing to the chants of the restless campesinos of Bolivia who were hungry for social reformation. A quartet of folk flutists accompanied the costumed dancers on stage, with a lead folk singer and guitarist getting the crowd on their feet with a rhythmic chant. A woman walked by distributing banners with Evo's face printed on the front . The colored newsprint read, "Bolivia. United, Grand and for All." I grabbed one and raised it above my head whilst jumping and shouting "Evo, Si!" I was either vehemently hated or deeply endeared by those of Bolivian nationality since many Morales administration policies were about breaking the bonds of United States political economic oppression disguised as developmental aid. Evo took the stage with his entire coalition to the cheers of us onlookers. He waited for the applause to subside and led the national anthem with his arm raised diagonally and hand flat. The entire entourage followed in similar fashion. In unison, the Plaza reverberated against the confining walls of the government palaces to create a resonating soliloquy of nationalist pride. He gave an acceptance speech in typical political fashion; short, catchy, and broadly defined, giving praise to the unity ahead. I had chills up my spine for 30 minutes that I fear I may never feel again for the same reasons in my own country. The magnificence had created a hunger inside me, both physically and emotionally. I had to satiate my physical hunger before anything else. The others agreed and we headed back to the hotel and ordered some delivery pizza for 50 Bolivianos.

Photo 12: Evo Morales (center balcony) with cabinet members, speaking to his indigenous base.

I saw a Dutch girl later that night in the hostel bar who had a beanie that she picked up earlier at the rally. It was blue with a white stripe, like the presidential flag, and on the brow it read, *Evo, Si!* I wanted it badly when I saw everyone else around me wearing cliché llama wool beanies in the typical tourist llama knit, complete with the chin straps hanging down. In my happiness I told her how it was the best beanie I'd ever seen. After asking me if I was serious, she offered it to me. I couldn't accept it without giving back something else. I ran into my room where I found my beanie I'd bought two years before while living in the Netherlands. It was simple: I'd take her beanie so long as she took mine to return to its proper place in her home country, where I'd bought it.

◎   ◎   ◎

After the rally, I was sure that I'd experienced the most original event of my travels. The indigenous makeup of the event and everyday life in Bolivia added to this sense of originality. Yet, the next day when I traveled to the famed pre-Inca relics of Tiwanaku, I encountered a particular item, no more than a few inches in height, that challenged my concept of what it really meant to be indigenous. Walking through the on-site museum I noticed a small pot molded into a face. It was very realistic and, due to its extreme realism, authentic in portraying a once-living individual. The man molded from clay had a Fu Machu mustache, a Japanese fishing hat, and narrow eyes. This artifact was found at the ruins and recorded the bust of an Asian man! My perspective on land rights and settlement patterns was immediately altered. Some anthropologists theorize that Japanese fishermen were blown off course to the coast of what was Bolivia and is now Chile, as early as 5,000 years ago. There are other convincing facts of Japanese settlement in the New World. Spanish conquistadors and other explorers noted that

Ecuadorian and Salomon Island natives had Japanese slaves. In the present day, there are reports of Japanese brigs washing up on the west coast of South America every few years. Trade winds would have made it difficult for Japanese sailors to go back across the Pacific Ocean, so it was unlikely that any settlement was intentional. Accidental settlement likely occurred sometime after Japan gained sea-going technology, which was around 3,000 BC. There was no doubt in my mind that this bust represented a Japanese man. Or should should I say native Bolivian? In my mind 5,000 year old accidental fishermen-cum-slaves, who were blown by wind, deserve more credit than 500 year old criminals-cum-conquistadors, who were lured by exploitation and gold.

But what classified someone as indigenous? Who had the right to land, be it for farming, natural resources, or religious purposes? This was the underlying controversy behind the reelection of the Evo Morales administration. I was an observer in a land I knew so little about. I had one more day in Bolivia and would then be heading to Isla de Sol, where the Inca religion is said to have arisen from the land. Interestingly enough, on Isla de Sol I would see that it wasn't the indigenous population that owned the island, but rather the slew of tourists. Arriving hourly by boat, they contributed to the island's tourist economy and left with the high altitude spirit.

8. Inca Origin

The bus ride to Copacabana was conducted past extensive terracing on the hillsides, which overcame the irregular contours ins successive horizontal uniformity. Dutch, German, and French created a multi-linguistic overtone within the tour bus, and it helped to drown out the hum of the poorly paved road below. There was a couple who spoke in English and I found out they were from Seattle. I was on a tourist bus and, unlike the other buses I took in the preceding weeks, it was full entirely of foreigners rather than a single card carrying Gringo— myself. It hadn't yet occurred to me that the trips I'd taken on the buses before were cut of most peoples' comfort zones. I booked this bus out of the ease of my hostel's travel agency. It was easy to pay for my trip just a few doors down from where my bed lie and the actual bus ride equaled the reservation process in effort: there was none. I was a paying tourist, and got what I paid for.

Our bus neared the shores of a lake and then left it behind. Just as I thought we'd turn and gone the opposite direction there was another lake in front of me. This happened three or four times as the bus careened around blind corners, following the same contours of the ever-present, ancient terracing both above and below the road. Looking at my map, I realized we were on a peninsula on the southeast bank of Lake Titicaca, the highest navigable lake in the world. The bus came down to lake level and entered a small town from the heights of the hills it had been navigating. A body of water presented itself ahead, but there wasn't a bridge or vessel clearly in sight. I was herded off the bus with my international peers. Would we swim? There was a small boat in sight but it didn't look like it could hold more than a fraction of the forty of us. Even if we made it across, what would happen with all of our packs, let alone our bus? We boarded the small boat and most people laughed uncomfortably as they snapped photos of our Tetris-packed predicament. The bus then drove onto a barge, which hadn't been clearly recognizable due to its pancake-like construction.

We made it over on our small water-going taxi and were filed past two customs soldiers via a slim pier. Passports were required, though mine remained locked in my backpack that was strapped to the top of the bus. I didn't think to bring it with me because both sides of the passage were on Bolivian land. Apparently, there was concern that Peruvians would boat to their side of the lake and hop onto the shoreline. In an effort to do what? I did not know. But it was concern enough for the two army green, fatigue-clad men to to instruct me to wait at the customs office, a small shack at the end of the pier. By that point the bus was back on solid ground and set to continue. What would be my first international noncompliance was disappointing and anti-climatic. I boarded the bus as I waited for a few of the Dutch tourists to buy some potato chips from a local vendor and we puttered along on our way.

My aspirations of handcuffed opposition to our forward progress were reignited briefly as we passed a naval checkpoint. Bolivia's only surviving Navy was based out of several ports within the landlocked lake since its coast had been taken by Chile more than a hundred years ago. A sailor in a pair of iron-pressed, though clearly old and fraying, dress whites stopped the bus only to wave it on through, after a brief glance at the papers.

Less than thirty minutes later we arrived in Copacabana, which rested in a small cove on the northwest end of the peninsula. Tourists were everywhere; this was the launching point for all Bolivian-initiated Titicaca adventures. I waited as my pack was thrown down from the roof rack of the tour coach by one of the bus operators, strapped my life to my back, and reconfirmed the daily notion that I did indeed pack too many things. I stumbled down the main street of the city, pulling my loose-fitting pants up repetitively and promising myself that I'd invest in a decent pair once I returned to the States, though I knew some good old American slacks would run significantly more than those ten dollar jeans. I was pleased because I knew these ten dollar Chilean jeans had to be down to a fractional cost of something like seven cents per wearing. The street leading down to the water was adorned with necklaces and earrings made by artisans. They were set on tables for any passing Gringo to buy. I made straight for the waterfront where I bought a ticket for the one o'clock boat to Isla del Sol. I had another hour to kill, so I made my way back up the same street, this time blowing past the eager jewelers, more focused on the food I needed to consume.

  I found a tourist café that was accessed by an alley, through the operating family's back porch where I mistakenly sat down. From there one had to travel up a staircase to an outdoor, rooftop patio. The Escher-staircase-like entrance spoke to the high demand for tourist commerce. Surely this cafe would never survive without the large tourist industry. It took me fifty minutes, out of the full hour I had until my boat departed, to get the tacos I'd ordered. The restaurant was a beacon for any hopeful business owner who wished to set up shop. It would not be hard to outdo. The tacos were minuscule at best and the guacamole on my plate was the consistency of Easy Cheese. I thumbed through my guidebook; I had to decide which hostel I'd stay in, on the island. I sat on the balcony, wrote, and thought about life. I was proud about how independent I'd become. At the other end of the small rooftop terrace a group of four Gringo guys sat and conversed over their glasses of beer. They were meeting to plan their day. It was around noon. Apparently we had the same guide. I could hear them read the description of the sustainable tourism hostel where I'd planned to stay. "Sustainable tourism? [Insert expletive here]," was what originally drew me into the conversation. But their ignorance hooked me when they went off on how little it took to become an educator, at any level, discrediting the profession as they consumed without regard on the high value of their dollar. These guys topped it as I left: they'd decided to continue their drinking and forget any goals for the day. It would be a *recovery* day for them. I threw on my 60-pound pack, paid with the little money I had, and went on to board the boat I'd reserved at the spur of the moment, only an hour ago. Patience, foresight and good intentions were with me. Effort had never entailed such great ease.

The boat crossing took nearly an hour. On one end of the lake was Peru, to my left, and Bolivia at my immediate right. The island to which we were heading appeared as a speck on the endless, blue lake horizon. I sat on the roof of the boat and felt the cool mountain air on my face. The boat puttered along at a rate just fast enough to create a small breeze and I subconsciously tightened my beanie.

The hour ride passed quickly and we arrived at the south end of the island. I left the boat, waited on the pier, and paid the first of a few island tolls, which although legit were nevertheless surprising. On a friend's suggestion, I found the Inca steps immediately, and headed straight up. I must have passed about fifty hostels on the way out of the tourist-rich corner of the island. It was no wonder why everyone aside from me decided to stay here: altitude and a 60-pound pack didn't compliment each other over the course of several hundred steps.

Each Inca step had an uncharacteristically long run. Surely few people close to my height had used this staircase when it was originally made because the average height of those who built the static escalator was five feet two inches. The stairs were used to accommodate pack llamas and any person who used it did so more easily on all fours, carrying their pack on a horizontally flat back. I knew this because it was the method I employed, due more to sheer exhaustion than ergonomics. I stopped several times to catch my breath, choking as any air I was capable of swallowing was sent back out before it had the chance to enter my lungs. From the Inca stairs I saw terraces jetting out in either direction; some full of gardens and others lying empty for perhaps hundreds of years. The agglomeration of hostels petered off, and so too did the heckling eight-year-olds who tried to get me and my pack into a residence for the night.

    I continued along for another couple of miles to the other end of the island, passing the northern tourism checkpoint and paying yet another entrance toll. I was assured it would be used for general archaeological upkeep. Then I hopped over some reconstructed ruins, that made up the base of a building, originally constructed by the Inca. This island, after all, had been the dominant religious center of the Inca. People had been here farming and constructing for thousands of years. Shortly after the northern checkpoint the trail became less discernible from the hillside. I looked at the rudimentary map on the back of my permit stub. It appeared as if the village on the northern end of the island was down the hill. In classic ill-fated fashion I decided to leave the trail. For my defense, I saw houses in the distance and figured that way would be a shortcut. I ascended the dry ground, from the island's peak, to a large patch of trees on the hillside and then wove between the farm plots, which followed the small forest.

Photo 13: *Terraces on the stepped Isla del Sol.*

After much confusion I emerged from a gully and into someone's backyard. In front of me stood four Aymara youngsters with blank stares and hanging jaws. I'd interrupted their outdoor play and was in a corner of the island where not many non-endemic traveled. I introduced myself to the children and laughed wryly when they kept pointing to my food. It was one thing for me to be generous and give gifts to every kid I saw and another thing for me to actually sustain myself. I had no extras! Feeling like I'd sincerely disappointed the children and eager to find the hostel, I bade them farewell.

I continued on between the brick walls of two neighboring animal pins, sure of my path for at least the next several hundred feet due to the constraint of the rock-wall pins on either side. I looked around for someone to ask for directions but the heat had forced everyone inside their homes. One man wandered by, intently marking a paper on a clipboard he held. I asked him for directions but he wasn't descriptive and, I sensed, tired of people like me. I zigzagged between animal pins, houses, outhouses, and small farm patches. An old man with a dozen sheep passed and offered a warm smile; a shepherd who wasn't bothered by the lost traveler, happy as long as his sheep followed him.

The muddy runoff that covered the path gave way to a sandy beach previously hidden from my view. A young family stood on the sand. There was a couple in their mid-twenties, their infant child who rested on the woman's back in a blanketed pouch and an older woman who was most definitely the grandmother of the baby. I was afraid I'd have to backtrack, since I couldn't see a hostel-like building anywhere around, and so I asked in suspense where it may be. The man and young woman responded in complimentary fashion, as the older woman looked on. The young lady with her child begged me to follow her and pointed a hundred yards distant, to the left and up a path on the hillside. There stood a building that looked much like a hostel. She pointed with a smile and demanded nothing. It was such a sharp contrast to the southern end of the island, where I'd been only a couple hours prior.

At the steps of the two story building, one of only a few multi-story structures throughout the island, I met yet another woman with a baby strapped to her back. She directed me to a large room with a couple of beds, a bathroom, and a lounge area. I threw down my bags and asked her where I needed to pay, check in, and get a key. She looked at me strangely and pointed to the key sitting in the door. Apparently the rest I need not worry about. I was exhausted and she informed me that dinner would be in a few hours. I could wait. I had no choice. I nibbled on some granola and went to read a book whose subject had something to do with alleviating global poverty.

The inch-wide book started with an introduction by Bono. The famed rocker's two syllable name was probably what caught my attention in the Copacabana travel store that morning, though I'd rather not confess that this is why I bought it. The book was written by Jeffrey Sachs, an economist who first rose to international fame when he used his theory of Shock Therapy to infuse the Bolivian economy with monetary aid in order to curb mass inflation. At the time he offered a convincing argument on how to alleviate poverty, but I would later read further into Latin American economic reform and discover that his strategy relied greatly on U.S. led IMF and World Bank intervention into the economies of the countries he 'turned around'. In fact, what he claimed to be economic aid was more aptly based on indentured servitude to U.S. economic policies, which relegated the receivers of the aid, like Bolivia, into a cycle of continuous borrowing to overcome debt and poverty. The cycle of lending instituted by foreign governments can be better described as capitalist exploitation; those benefiting from capitalism are inherently dependent on a much larger population that's worse off, and will continue to be. Sachs' good intentions didn't see Bolivia's desire to give something more back to itself in the form of social services, as a monetary return from it's vast natural resources. That cycle was inescapable until Evo Morales became president. His cabinet found a way out by breaking IMF/World Bank ties and canceling remaining debt with the help of multilateral relief.

    I looked up from my book and watched as shepherds guided their animals along the beach, presumably returning from a day of grazing. This was why all the pens I'd passed earlier had been empty. The animals followed their shepherd at a removed distance, as if they needed no guiding, and undoubtedly fell into the same routine each evening. A cow would lead, followed by a donkey or two, then a few sheep and a couple of goats. I wondered, did this order had anything to do with the cranial capacity of the animals? They formed a single file line and treaded over the sand which buffered the water line; hard enough to walk on but dry enough to be comfortable. Five more sets of animals, all without shepherd, followed the same path. I could hear the waves beating on the shore.

The wind was giving me a chill so I grabbed a sweater from my room and decided I would walk along the stretch of beach with my camera. When I returned I saw some women standing on the the deck near me. They'd arrived earlier and were staying in the next room. After talking for a while in Spanish I soon figured out one spoke rudimentary English! But this was bad, since I needed more Spanish practice. One of the girls, Priscilla, and I took a short walk on the beach as the sun went down. We found a small store that had some very basic supplies and one, yes one, bottle of wine left. Unfortunately, I had no money on me and the man was closing up for the evening. There had to be another way to get an evening drink.

We headed back to the hostel and sat down with some playing cards at the dinner table, which was in an adjacent building to the lodge. Dinner was served over the course of an hour. Our hostess juggled three kids while fixing up a quinoa dish and hot soup. The oldest child, a girl probably eleven, served us. Upon learning they had beer I eagerly asked the eleven-year-old to bring me a bottle and didn't feel the least bit awkward about it. With the beer, altitude, long day of hiking, and food digesting I became tired very fast. I made plans with Priscilla to go to some Inca ceremonial ruins the next day. The ruins were further north on the tip of the island and it would be a couple hours walking with my full pack.

My room was dark and extremely cold. I fell asleep imagining the ghosts of past Inca watching over me. The full moon crept through a small window, breaking the black mold of night. The twilight brought altitude and fatigue induced visions, dare I say dreams, of ancient Inca specters. I perspired constantly under the many layers of blankets and awoke, in the morning, with the chills and ready for a shower.

Photo 14: *A shepherd and her sheep follow a cow away from the beach to higher pastures.*

The sun was breaking over the horizon and I wanted to beat any backpackers to the ruins so I forwent the shower. Instead, I partook in the standard breakfast of bread, jam, butter and instant coffee to drink. Afterwards I packed my things, and paid. There was still no sign of Priscilla and I finished tightening my pack straps on a brick wall, readjusting them by my side for optimal comfort. Did she speak with drunken sincerity? I bent down to gain the momentum needed to hoist on my pack, then out of the far hostel door emerged the girl I'd talked to the night before. She'd slept in and asked me if I could wait for ten minutes.

Soon we headed down to the beach and up through the other end of the small village where a patch of woods began. We began the days hike with an exchange of life stories in a mixed lexicon. She was from Ecuador and was working on her college degree. It had something to do with environmental engineering, judging by the little I understand. My pack was growing heavy and I tried not to show it but my long hair tightened up and I could feel the sweat flowing down the individual helix of each curl.

While walking along we passed some different stock animals - a donkey, a cow, creatures I could see eye to eye with. But when a noise couldn't readily be identified within the horizontal plane of my eyes, I became curious where it came from. I inspected my peripheral vision in an effort to find a persistent grunting sound, but nothing. Then, looking down, I saw a little piglet. He was about the size of my head, completely brown in color, and was walking back and forth. I had to pick up the little guy and when I lifted him I realized his grunt was nothing compared to the loud squealing that ensued. My pack was heavy and I wanted to get to the ruins so I put him back down after a brief photo op. I continued on only to realize his 400-pound mom was around the corner, staring at me but luckily tied by a rope to a stake. The piglet followed Priscilla and I down the weaving path for a good five minutes and only turned back after he reached some changing turf that represented the end of his known world.

We eventually made it to another toll collecting point, which sat just before the ruins. This time I avoided the fee thanks to Priscilla. It helped to be traveling with an attractive and amiable Spanish-speaking woman. She talked at length with the toll collector. At the ruins, there was a large sacrificial table, which was made out of one solitary stone slab measuring about 20 inches thick. It was used for llama sacrifice. Several smaller stones were positioned around the slab. I imagined that they were used as seats for the priests administering the sacrifice. There were extensive stone ruins on the slope of the hill below the altar and a rock up hill that was shaped like a cougar's mouth. We explored both. I kept wearing my bag, for lack of a better place to store it. I couldn't avoid hitting the top of the low door frames that connected the rooms of the old structure.. The ruins must have been a royal palace. I looked down at the placid blue water and imagined an Inca going for a swim on a sunny day with a clear blue sky, much like the day at hand. From here the Inca had a view of the greater part of the lake to the north and could easily participate in religious ceremonies. On the island it was also the furthest place away from the mainland and provided a solid military position because of this location.

After exploring the ruins and eating granola for a bit we headed down to a village on the northern end of the island, bought lunch and caught a boat back to Copacabana that saved a half-day walk with my pack. I was one of a few backpackers who'd brought their pack onto the island. I'd heard that most people left their luggage at a locker in Copacabana or at a hostel on the south end of the Isla del Sol. But that took money and travel plans. I didn't have either. I took in the view of the Andean Cordillera which encapsulated the Lake Titicaca. People talked and I sat, watched and breathed in the magnificently fresh air evaporating, in the heat, off the lake's aqueous surface. The afternoon was slow in Copacabana and I spent most of it eating while waiting for the night bus which would take me out of Bolivia and into Peru.

Since I'd arrived in Bolivia a month earlier, my understanding of Spanish as a foreign language improved and my capacity to understand other cultures grew widely. It was ironic, then, when these two capabilities reached a new nadir, just as I was leaving the country. After a few expected setbacks at the border, that had to do with missing stamps and subsequent fines by other travelers on the shuttle, it was onward into the night. The shuttle needed to make the connection in the first large Peruvian city, Puno, so that everyone could arrive in Cuzco by morning. In the ten-person shuttle there was a driver, a guide, two middle-aged couples, three Dutch students, and myself. The students and I ended up talking throughout the length of the trip at normal pace and volume in our common language, which was English.

The man, in the couple sitting closest to the students and I calmly, but sternly, turned around and asked us to speak slowly. It was an odd request and so none of us paid too much attention. We talked on for what seemed like another three-quarters of an hour until the guy turned around, no longer calm, and yelled at the top of his lungs, "Speak SLOWLY!!" In all honesty, we never slowed down our conversation since he first asked so he had every right to be frustrated. I was sure, however, that there were better means of asking to be included. Again, he yelled and begged simultaneously, "Speak SLOWLY!!" This time he pushed one of the Dutch students. Everyone was paying attention now. A new level of inquisitiveness ensued and we realized he meant for us to speak softer. Fair enough, but what was with all the hitting and yelling? Based on his accent I guessed the irreverent man was speaking Portuguese, which meant he was probably a Brazilian tourist. I was even more confused now because I'd always imagined Brazilians to be laid back; ready to chat, make music and party. I was still rather complacent about the situation as none of his remarks were directed to me, though that changed fast. He turned around, grabbed my shoulders and began shaking me while yelling, "Slowly, slowly, SLOWLY!" The man had a serious language barrier, a real Napoleonic complex coupled with travel anxiety and soon-to-be serious issues with his marriage, as I saw his wife cringe in embarrassment. I grabbed the fool and pushed him off. The force of my instinctual push was enough to throw him but his seatbelt assured he didn't go to far. Then, I made it very clear that he wouldn't touch me again and that he would kindly mind his own business. He retorted with some jabs at my juvenile demeanor and I was happy to tell him how much more mature my fifth grade students had been. If he wanted quiet then he should have never traveled to such an inspiring place, where one is compelled to speak of the sublime and regard nature's wonder with awe.

So I beg of you, inspired reader and hopefully soon to be traveler. Don't let the man get you down. He'll try telling you *slowly*, but his intention is to quiet you all together. He'll tell you to get off the road, but remember to keep facing forward. When it's not safe he'll start to shake but that shouldn't affect you. And when he's nervous he'll yell, but for you that's of no consequence. Is he gonna quiet you or are you gonna push back? You've seen places and things that you've never expected and now the road ahead is the same as when you started: unknown.

9. Epilogue: Back in the States

The following is selected journal entries, poetry, and musings from my first months back in the United States. The necessity to earn money, the purpose of life behind cubicle walls, and figuring out where I'd head next with a job, school or travel occupied my mind after the freedom and nominal budgetary needs I lived off of during the previous months.

Sept 3rd, 2008

I finished my iced tea, which cost me two dollars. Two bucks; cheap for American standards but too expensive for the guy who recently returned from South America. Before I would've bought a couple cookies to snack on, but now just felt like they'd be weighing me down. Since returning to America, my Mother had felt it her personal duty to fatten me up any way she could. I had a steady diet of trail mix cookies, burritos, BBQ dinners (though that one can be credited to Dad) and milk. Most of this food I felt wasn't necessary as I ate out of boredom rather than the hunger produced from carrying a 60-pound pack at 4,000 meters ASL. Here I was in a coffee shop in the middle of Silicon Valley, full of business meetings and laptops at 5:26 PM, well beyond the end of any Latin-American workday. People here had an excess of money, which I could see as I watched the woman next to me compare prices of new cell phones on her laptop as she simultaneously blocked calls on her current mobile phone. It seemed like a new number would be the easier way out, but then I remembered I was in the digitally encapsulated Silicon Valley, where it was much easier to stylishly flow down the circuit's lines that covered the Valley's silicon walls rather than cut yourself off from them.

Sept 14th, 2008

I sat down in downtown Palo Alto on a Sunday evening at Peet's Coffee. I thought it would be more bustling here than in Mountain View, but after five minutes I think I've been proven wrong. I walked into Starbucks not wanting to frequent the place I despise most, but realized I wouldn't have to; the store didn't have WiFi. I don't think I need WiFi to write and it may have been nice to sit there. A girl was reading, "The Spirit Catches You and You Fall Down," which I read in college for a health systems class. It would have been nice to discuss. But why else would I want to be there? To buy the same tasting vanilla latte that I drank in Santiago or London? Was it because I had money on a Starbucks card? That was probably it. Then I went to Peet's and I was glad. They gave me the WiFi code and a free drip coffee. I was refreshed by such kindness.

Last night was a big welcome back party for me. I showed my slides, which I really hated doing. I didn't like the attention on myself. I got through them quickly though, whoever wanted to listen was welcome to do so, and whoever wanted to eat or talk could do that. I directed a multiple dish meal that started with buying tomatoes and peppers at the Mountain View farmer's market. I made sopaipillas, humitas and pebre salsa. My family helped me out with salmon and Chilean style chicken. Everyone loved the food. Melinda helped with some music. Eric helped with some pisco sours. Aunt Missy and Uncle Jeff were in Napa and came down for a couple hours to surprise everyone. Mom screamed and we all thought she had burnt herself but was really just surprised to see my Aunt. Grandma, Grandpa, and Uncle John all came up from Simi Valley, California. It was nice to see everyone and to know that I had their support, though I feel I'm past the point in my life of needing it. I want some friends around here, which is why I went to the coffee shop to write. I need friends like the ones I met the last few months on the road. It's such a contrast but I'll recover. I'm in a valley, which is natural I suppose, because I just came down from a peak. But a valley lies in between two peaks. So here I go climbing.

Sept 23rd, 2008

My voice between the transfers,
the lines repeat, but the borders undefined.
Where does the work end and reality begin?
Surely someone must think this life to be the real truth.

Outside, I walk through the planters, trampling one flower at a time:
Islands of hope in this corporate abyss.
I continue to the parking lot; a hollow sea.
The asphalt radiates with oil trying to escape, but bounded together by the cool bay heat.

The supervisor in charge of temporary workers instructs me: "What we do is sell short wave radios. W are the sole supplier to the Red Cross."
Most of the calls I receive are from people who have a warranty issue with their radio:
In a thick Southern accent, "Yes, I ummm have a radio, ahhh here."
[Yes, you do]
"And well ah you see it decided to stop working."
[Bad radio!]
"I had a warranty on it..."
I say, "Let me connect you to our tech department."
"But I need to talk to the warranty folks!"
I counter, "Our technical department also covers warranty"
"Ughh fine th---".
My finger on the transfer switch cuts them off.

In the background I hear lawn equipment but all I see are the untrimmed swaths of grass: green, but pale where the sun manages to reach beyond the shade of carefully-planted deciduous. The contrast in the concrete bordered plot is amazing. Checkered by carefully-cubed hedges and bulbous perennials, the sagely swath continues skyward, each blade cutting off another for vertical supremacy.

I think of my backyard grass, struggling in drought and about to rot while the sagely swath, decked in its plush green blades, looks at the shoes of the business masses. It says, "go on your own way, you have no need to run barefoot here. I was made to be looked at. That brown at home is where you ought to trot."

Oct 10th, 2008

My mornings no longer consist of waking up to strange faces over Nescafe and bread bun breakfasts, nor do they entail carrying a 60-pound pack with all my possessions to the next bus or bed.

Now I'm given the luxury of actual drip coffee, rather than the Nescafe mix so prevalent in South America. Ironically, it was the only option, at the cheap residences I frequented, in a continent where over 50% of the world's coffee comes from. Likewise, I'm no longer limited to street bread, some of which is very tasty despite its mysterious origins, but now consume seven-grain bran cereal on a regular basis; five of which I'm sure are native cereals to the southern continent.

My mornings consist of a bike ride that zigzags through the gridded streets of my parent's peri-urban neighborhood. How do you say bedroom community in Spanish? I feel a sense of protection as I raise my hands up and off the handlebars while biking, to stretch and breathe deeply. The only danger I face is avoiding the young kids crossing the street for elementary school, but there is a crossing guard to protect both parties involved.

On the arterial street I swerve in the bike lane to avoid branches that were cut the day before by city pruners. Perhaps they were encroaching on a power line; the one I never notice because my gaze is focused on the road ahead. Each successive day I seem to have one more dead squirrel to avoid; splattered on the pavement, pancake flat today, crepe thin tomorrow. It's easy for me to play Pinkerton and decipher from their thickness which is the new kid, literally, on the block.

It's easy to forget about what is old and look to the future as I turn onto Charleston Rd. and pass Google Dr. The next six and a half minutes of the ride are through the Google campus. There's a mellow vibe that I think stems from the lack of vehicle traffic, thanks to the shuttle that carries around the googly-eyed employees. I'm sure that after twelve hours in front of a computer there's some truth to the appellation of the Google faithful as googly-eyed. I'll never bike home this way because of their skewed vision, lest I want to end up like my squirrel friends. I see some cars too and put myself in their shoes: never mind that biker on the side of the road, that's not progress like a hybrid car. Because they are logged on to their in-car mapping system they'll probably never see me riding until I'm just another squirrel.

Oct 27th, 2008

My job duties consist of answering the phones at a tech company for maybe eight minutes, on a busy day. That's between one and two percent of my eight hour workday. Now the day after my birthday I was in an office and lonesome with lack of recognition. No one knew it was my birthday yesterday. It gave me a lot of time to think about things and people.

Lately I found myself doing the most obscure things so that my mind would have a little free time from thinking about a girl I knew. When I played guitar, carefully aligning my voice with the steady rhythm of the chord progressions, was I singing about her? When I was planting my garden, biking to work, and volunteering for the Obama campaign was I doing them I liked to or were these things I did to bolster my resume with the female species?

I realized that I should buy into activities and qualities that I admired in others; only then would I see the personal rewards for myself. There was a certain part of me which secretly knew that when you actualize your life by investing in certain ideas, interests, and movements, you become the person which others of similar existential needs aspire to be. Was I looking for myself? Was someone else looking for themselves? Would we find ourselves together or secretly wax and wane between desire for each other's self? Or would we be trapped in our tunnel vision, naturally, to pursue our own interests without realizing there was someone right beside us?

Escapism from the self, desire for what one cannot have or be: this is the essence of attraction. But I didn't want to buy into this. I desire nothing more than a woman who is free of all guilt, regret, repression, rules, and for lack of a better explanation, reason. To me the only thing that makes sense in a woman is that which makes no sense at all. For if I really understood someone then how would that be escaping?

As much as I was escaping from the humdrum of my eight-minute-a-day work life to imagine serene landscapes, I didn't want the images of her to be misconstrued for a desire to escape boredom. She was on a schedule, hardly sleeping, working ten hour days and biking to work while I was doing laps around the cubicles and sitting my butt down in the car to drive home. I desired her lifestyle and her tenacity. I wanted to be in a new and foreign place. I wanted to be away from everything I knew and to get out of my element. I only knew that the future was unknown.

Oct 30th, 2008

I love the smell of car heaters, especially in the fall. Particularly that moment when you get into your cold car. It could be morning and you'd be dashing from your front door over the broken red leaves and jumping into the car only to realize it's even colder than outside. It could be on a lunch break as you're driving to get a burrito on an overcast day. It could be as you're driving back from the bar, two or three beers deep with your muffled senses comforted by the subtle heat.

No other experience reminds me more of a Toyota Corolla and it's heater/defroster, which I owned before going to South America, than the Toyota Camry and it's heater/defroster, which I owned now. Recirculated life. Reinvigoration. A wake up call to the past. All fall's leaves ground up into the aromatics of the musty, decade old tubing. I was left with one question: was I smelling the fall in Japan from production year 1995? Or was this fall in California?

Nov 4th, 2008

I woke up at 5:30 AM today so that I could go in and make calls for Obama starting at six. I was up until about 11:30 last night. I didn't need much sleep because I ran a 5K and worked out a bunch at the gym. Being active always helps me sleep better. I wanted to get in shape for the Turkey Trot, but just found out that I will probably go to Colorado instead! Aunt Missy emailed me today asking if I'd like to come out there to help chop some wood at the cabin and do a little boarding. I'm stoked to go to the mountains, cut down some trees, and breathe in the mountain air. It will be good and I can still keep up on the workout thing.

Anyway, I was amazed at how many people were at the campaign calling center; more than 100 at 6:00 AM. Apparently this call center leads the nation in calls per day and it's entirely a grassroots station. That is, it's not a headquarters or satellite office. Nationwide, more than one million people have made calls throughout the campaign. Americans are politically involved!

I was able to leave work for a little bit at lunch and voted over at St. Timothy's church down the street from my parent's place, where there was no line! I walked right in and voted next to my neighbor. In the parking lot of the voting station, I was given a flier for Prop 8 that said 'Vote No' and happily accepted. I want gay marriage to stay legal because it's a basic civil/human rights issue about people being treated equally and fair. If they can't marry, then we are discriminating against them just as if they had an interracial marriage. How archaic is that? In my mind Prop 8 is the most important issue aside from the Presidential election on this year's ballot. It has set records for the amount of money spent by both sides in advertising campaigns, for or against it, to ever go on a ballot.

My Dad just called to talk about the elections. I'm sitting at work, typing this and waiting until about 4:30 so I can leave to make some more last minute calls, though at that time all of the East Coast and most contentious states will be closed. I think we'll focus on Nevada and maybe even Alaska. What a great information age we live in. I'm going to watch the race come to a close at the Palo Alto for Obama location, where I'll be making phone calls, and then I'll head to downtown Palo Alto for a few drinks. Here's to a hopeful four years!

Nov 5th, 2008

So, so, so tired from making phone calls before and after work yesterday. But even more tired from all the partying I did last night. We won! I made it to the bar just as Senator McCain was conceding the election and had to watch it from the line outside. I finally got in and ordered a tower of beer just in time to see Obama come on television in front of a crowd of tens of thousands in Chicago and millions watching from across the country. I'm getting chills up my spine just thinking about the experience of watching him get elected. And the best thing is that I know I'm not alone. I watched as the bar stood silent and the waitresses stopped serving drinks so that they could watch the T.V. screens like everyone else. The remainder of the crowd waiting outside had their eyes fixed on the flat screens. No one talked. I drank beer and listened intently. I she a tear of joy or two. My friend told me that it was because of me, which meant a lot to hear from someone and especially from her. I didn't think I deserved any special praise but it felt good because I'd worked for it. I was back home and things were going to change - I could feel it.

www.ingramcontent.com/pod-product-compliance
Lightning Source LLC
Chambersburg PA
CBHW032000080426
42735CB00007B/460